1985

ROADS

*"More miracles are wrought by prayer than this world dreams of.,,*

Alfred Lord Tennyson

CLARICE BRUNO

# ROADS TO PADRE PIO

Third edition

1970

Printed in Italy by Città Nuova - Rome
© 1969 N. I/165198 by Clarice Bruno

First edition: November 1969
Second edition: February 1970
Third edition: May 1970

*Nihil obstat:* Fr. Ferdinand Galea ofm
Rome, February 10, 1970
*Imprimatur:* † Aloysius Liverzani, Episcopus Tusculanus
Frascati, February 16, 1970

# TABLE OF CONTENTS

7

# In Tribute

*A little page upon which to pause . . .*
*. . . and remember*
*My Sacred Heart Convent days at*
*Lake Forest, Illinois . . . as well as*
*my final two College years at*
*Rosemont College, in Pennsylvania.*
*Impossible to thank for all the*
*" Good Seed " so deeply planted . . .*
*If it took a long time to begin maturing*
*the fault was only mine!*
*The air breathed in those walls*
*. . . the example given . . . IRREPLACEABLE*
*My appreciation only grows with the years.*

*A young Padre Pio*

Part I

# PADRE PIO

# A Few Biographical Words.

This book is not a biography of Padre Pio. It presupposes that most persons are cognizant of the main facts of his life, so many books and articles having already been written concerning him. However, it is hoped that something of the essential and vital in Padre Pio can be mystically gleaned from the sum total of these pages so that the reader will be able, to some extent at least, to discover him deductively.

For those who are still totally uninformed regarding him, these few pages have been added and will of necessity be brief, including only a few facts relevant to his long life, while Padre Pio can really only be found in the thousand-and-one details and nuances that are " between the lines ".

We find some consolation, however, in the words of Lorenzo Patri:

" We note that in all the books already written concerning Padre Pio, from the most pretentious and voluminous, to the smallest and most modest, all have been able to reveal only an infinitesimal part of the complete figure of the Capuchin. To

write about Padre Pio would require another
Padre Pio. " *

Padre Pio was born in 1887, in Pietrelcina in the
province of Benevento, not many miles from Naples. The
house in which he, as well as the other four children
of the family, was born, was small and modest, his
parents being poor country folk, dedicated to farming.
This little house had, however, a great richness:
externally, an immense horizon and view of the undulat-
ing green valley below, and, internally, a united, loving,
and truly Christian family, wherein the spirit of self-
sacrifice was almost limitless. His mother began each
day prayerfully in church, imploring the strength and
guidance necessary for her maternal duties. His father,
who labored long hours daily, caring for his land and
sheep, was later to emigrate twice to America, painfully
separating himself from his loved ones in order to earn
the money to pay for the studies of Francesco, later
to become Padre Pio. Francesco's first teacher was a
neighboring peasant who taught the child to read and
write. Eventually, because he proved such an apt pupil,
his education was entrusted first to the parish priest,
and then to the village teacher.

But lessons and books were too costly for the small
family purse and so Francesco's father departed alone to
face the distant, solitary and difficult life of the emigrants
of that era in order to provide the means for his son's
education.

* Patri, Lorenzo, *Cenni Biografici di Padre Pio,* (carries Imprimatur).

As for Francesco, he was a docile and meditative child, precociously aware spiritually. At the age of five, he tells us that he had already pledged fidelity to St. Francis of Assisi; at the age of nine his mother was to discover him attempting to sleep on the cold, hard floor, with a stone for a pillow.

In Francesco, intelligence and spirituality grew hand in hand. Once, upon his mother's asking how the boy was getting on, the teacher had answered, " Eh, Giuseppa, I don't know what more to teach the boy, he knows more than I do. " And later, when a student in the Franciscan seminary, upon his mother's query, again the reply, " ... it is as though he did not exist, he is so far ahead of us all "—meaning in virtue as well as in study, for his extreme humility and serenity in all circumstances, even the most painful, have always characterized Padre Pio. During his student years, he suffered from very poor health, repeatedly recovering suddenly and inexplicably, from serious illnesses, much to everyone's amazement. When in the seminary, he moved from convent to convent, from Morcone to San Elia a Piansi, where he finished his high school studies, to Montefusco for philosophy and theology.

At that time, seminarians were sent to Benevento for the Cardinal's oral examination. " Piuccio, you cannot go," said his superior. " You have been ill, and therefore are not prepared." " I will join the others even if I have to go on foot," he replied. He was given permission to accompany his classmates in a horse-drawn cart. In the ensuing examination before the Cardinal, Francesco finished first in his class.

He was already completely consumed by his love of God and it was this total dedication to Christ, coupled with his virtue, which placed him, even at this early age, in a spiritual category greatly advanced beyond that of his fellow novices.

Throughout his days, all his thoughts and desires had but one point of reference—the dawning of his day of ordination to the priesthood. On one occasion, when asked if he had slept well, he replied, " And who can sleep when one's heart is bursting with joy? "

Soon after ordination, he was sent from his monastery to his parent's home in Pietrelcina because of the delicate state of his health. Here he remained for a few years as assistant to the old parish priest, Don Panullo who was to become his good friend and confidant, and who intuitively understood the already matured saintliness of his young colleague. Francesco, now Padre Pio, spent hours of prayer in church, and was frequently seen to be in ecstacy when at the altar celebrating the Holy Sacrifice of the Mass. It is from Don Panullo that we have learned a great deal regarding this period of Padre Pio's life.

Don Panullo also knew of the insidious, diabolical torments to which Padre Pio was subjected and once said consolingly: " Piuccio, it is Our Lord who wants and permits this in order to temper you and to strengthen you." To no one else, outside of this paternal priest, did Padre Pio confide his mystical life and experience.

It was during this stay at Pietrelcina, we are told, that he received the Stigmata in its first, invisible stage.

In 1916, Padre Pio was called into military service as a chaplain. He was stationed in a hospital in Naples but instead of assisting the sick, the doctors hastened to assist him, finding the young priest in a most depleted state of health. These doctors soon arranged for his discharge from military service when they were unable to combat, successfully, the fearfully high temperatures which threatened to shatter their thermometers.

His Franciscan superiors then sent him to the convent in Foggia, transferring him soon afterward to San Giovanni Rotondo, where it was hoped that the good air (500 meters above sea level) would help to restore his health. This proved a difficult task because of the effect of the still invisible stigmata, and the terrifying, diabolical torments of this period.

1916 was the year of Padre Pio's arrival at San Giovanni Rotondo, and never since then has he moved from this little sanctuary dedicated to Our Lady of Divine Grace. Here he passed the next two years, humbly hidden from the eyes of the world, engulfed in prayer and penance, and enraptured in his love and devotion to Christ crucified.

On September 20, 1918, his fellow monks found Padre Pio unconscious and bleeding before the large crucifix in the choir loft of the little church. Now the five wounds of the stigmata were clearly visible; his hands and feet perforated as though by nails, just as were those of Our Divine Lord upon the cross, and his side pierced, a reproduction of the wound caused by the soldier's lance after Christ's death. This event is still hidden by a mysterious veil, through which we are not as yet permitted to see.

September of 1968 therefore, marks the fiftieth year that Padre Pio has carried these five bleeding wounds, which have never changed, never healed, never become infected. It would be useless to go into a long dissertation on this point. What would speak more eloquently than these fifty years during which pure and perfumed blood has constantly flowed from the five wounds? I will only add a few words and observations made by Doctor Festa who was commissioned by Roman ecclesiastical authorities to examine these wounds, and to find a scientific explanation, if there was one. Doctor Festa examined Padre Pio, with the assistance of other doctors. He concluded that there could be no justifiable scientific explanation, since all evidence was completely contrary to the laws of nature. This he demonstrated in such a way as to challenge all doubt. We quote, (translated from the Italian):

> " All the five wounds observed in Padre Pio are to be considered real and true anatomical wounds of the tissues, whose persistent continuation, whose strange anatomical, pathological characteristics, with their capacity for continuous bleeding, with the blood always fresh and perfumed, and their locality corresponding exactly to the parts of the body that Our Lord suffered as a holocaust in His crucifixion may constitute a mystery, but only for him who from the tangible evidence that nature so generously proffers does not rise to the synthetic grandeur of our religion and faith. " *

* Festa, *Misteri Di Scienza E Luci Di Fede,* p. 51.

A good number of years after his first visit, Doctor Festa found the five wounds in the same condition, adding:

> " These are the only wounds on Padre Pio's person, the skin on the rest of his body presenting itself with all the characteristics of absolute and perfect integrity. "

Another physician, Doctor Romanelli, narrates that, having visited San Giovanni Rotondo for the first time, he noticed that a certain fragrance emanated from the person of Padre Pio. He observed: " .... Strange indeed that a monk held in such high spiritual regard should use perfume. " He also had occasion to note the same fragrance on a staircase before leaving, and wrote to the Provincial that " it was not autosuggestion, because no one had ever spoken to me of this phenomenon. " He declared, " It is too simple and habitual to attribute always to autosuggestion, phenomena which we do not know how to explain in any other way. "

Doctor Festa further narrates that this perfume emanates directly from the blood that flows from the wounds and describes an episode which happened to him:

> " In my first visit to Padre Pio, I removed from the wound on his side a gauze filled with blood, which I took away with me enclosed in a small case, intending to examine it later under a microscope ... An officer and other persons with whom I shared a taxi on the return trip, despite the ventilation in the speeding automobile, and

ignorant of the case containing the gauze which I carried with me, all became aware of the fragrance, and assured me it corresponded to the perfume that emanated from the person of Padre Pio. In the days following my arrival in Rome, and for a long period of time, this same piece of gauze, kept in a cabinet in my office, so thoroughly perfumed the room, that many patients spontaneously asked me the origin." *

If we consider the repugnant odor of even fresh blood, we must conclude, with Doctor Festa, that " this phenomena, in its complete simplicity, and with the eloquence with which it presents itself to our study, is therefore contrary to any natural scientific law, surpassing all that is logical or debatable, and we, in all honesty, cannot but observe and admit this reality."

Later, this same doctor operated on Padre Pio for a hernia which healed in a completely normal manner. Padre Pio refused anesthesia and, due to the ensuing pain, lost consciousness for a few minutes during and after the operation. Dr. Festa took advantage of one of the lapses to re-examine the stigmatic wounds which appeared to him, after a period of many years, identical to those of the youthful examination. Moreover, the wound on Padre Pio's side could be clearly seen and presented itself in the form of a cross, " with brief, but evident, radiations of light that emerged from its contours." Dr. Merla of San Giovanni Rotondo, who

* Festa, op. cit., pp. 159 and 177.

was also present, noted the same manifestation, speaking of it often to his patients.

As to Padre Pio's daily way of life during all these years, I will again quote Lorenzo Patri:

" His nutrition is very meager. Only once in twenty-four hours does he join his Franciscan brothers in refectory, tasting only a little soup and a bit of vegetable. Despite his limited nourishment and rest, the trying hours spent in the confessional and in intense prayer, not to mention the constant suffering caused by his bleeding wounds, his intellectual energy and strength of will are magnificent, and his being able to persist in all this enormous work from early morning until late at night, can only fill us with wonder . . . . When he finally lies down, it is only to remain in his bed for a few hours."

The truly great charm of Padre Pio is in the way the supernatural walks arm in arm with the most disarming naturalness and simplicity.

Let us hope that the 50th anniversary of his stigmatization, his long mission of suffering and prayer will open the skies and shower the world, so in need of guidance, with abundant spiritual blessings.

We will conclude with the words spoken by Pope Benedict XV to Bishop Damiani (Salto Uruguay): " Padre Pio is one of those truly extraordinary persons whom God sends from time to time to convert men."

*Bi-Location.*

A few words on this mysterious subject. Of the fact there is no doubt, too many people of all walks of life, type, and intelligence having had the experience of seeing Padre Pio bi-located.

A monk, speaking of the bi-location of St. Anthony of Padua, observed, " Maybe these souls so privileged by Our Lord are not even aware of when their bi-location happens." Padre Pio, hearing this, interrupted in a lively manner, as one already well acquainted with such things. He said, " Of course they are aware of what is happening. They may not know if it is their body or their soul that is moved, but they are well conscious of what is taking place, and they know where they are going."

Of the many instances reported in connection with Padre Pio, I shall mention only three.

Monsignor Damiani, Vicar-General of the Diocese of Salto, Uruguay, already cured of cancer through the prayers of Padre Pio, remarked while on a visit to San Giovanni Rotondo that when he died he would have wished to be assisted by his friend Padre Pio, but Padre Pio told him he would die in Uruguay, not in San Giovanni Rotondo. Whereupon the prelate entreated so insistently that Padre Pio promised to be near him on his deathbed.

On the occasion of the anniversary of the ordination of Monsignor Alfredo Viola in 1941, all the bishops of Uruguay were together in the house of the diocesan bishop and among these was Monsignor Damiani who

was suffering from angina pectoris. Towards midnight, His Excellency, the Bishop of Montivideo, Monsignor Antonio M. Barbieri, awakened, having heard someone knock on his door and, because it was partly open, he was able to see a monk passing in the corridor. At the same moment, he heard a murmuring voice say, " Go to Monsignor Damiani's room." The prelate hurriedly put on some clothing and, after having awakened other bishops and priests, he went with them to Monsignor Damiani's room. He arrived in time to administer the last sacraments. What amazed them all was a note written by Monsignor Damiani before he died. It contained these words: " Padre Pio came."

Another incident also seems worth recording. At the end of World War I, in 1918, General Cadorna, in a moment of great anguish, noticed a strong scent of perfume near him, and glimpsed a monk who spoke a few words of comfort and then disappeared. On the advice of a Franciscan, the general went to San Giovanni Rotondo dressed in civilian clothes, and without having told anyone of his plans. Two monks presented themselves to the general saying that Padre Pio was waiting for him.*

And, one more incident. Doctor Sala, the socially and professionally prominent heart specialist, left a large Northern Italian city and, as a result of a great grace granted through Padre Pio's intercession—the cure of his seriously ill child—established himself at San

---

* De Robeck, Nesta, " Padre Pio Apostolo della Chiesa " (Imprimatur).

Giovanni Rotondo. Doctor Sala is a veritable gold mine of anecdotes regarding Padre Pio, having become in the last ten years of Padre Pio's life, one of his most personal friends and doctors.

It is impossible in this particular book that aims at giving only a sample, brief touches of the many sides of Padre Pio, even to begin unwinding this long, fascinating spool. Perhaps another time. Because of its briefness, one amusing little account.

Doctor Sala traverses the church square late one night when to his surprise he sees Padre Pio making his way toward the convent entrance. " Good evening, Padre Pio " he calls. He receives no answer. Padre Pio passes calmly through the unopened door and disappears. The next day when visiting him, Doctor Sala says: " Padre, I saw you outside on the square last night but when I greeted you, you did not answer." " Oh," says Padre Pio apologetically, " evidently I didn't hear you."

Part II

# MY ROAD

## " TRY TO REMAIN UNDER GOD'S GAZE AND GOD WILL ALWAYS BEAR YOU WITNESS."

These are the words Padre Pio spoke to me spontaneously at the end of a confession some years ago, and it is upon these words—upon my belief in their complete integrity—that this book is based.

One of the rules of the Third Order of St. Francis is to make a will, early and clearly.

While thinking of my family and material things, I began thinking of things of a spiritual order, of all the graces granted to me, and friends, through Padre Pio's intercession and prayers. I decided to put at least some of these on paper to leave as a sort of spiritual testament. I did not want to die leaving so much " light hidden under a bushel," as the Gospel says . . . .

At this point, Padre Pio's words, quoted above, returned to my mind. If, in all sincerity, I did my best to write all things with honesty, as though God were gazing at my words, He would alwaye bear witness! And, if

* His exact words in Italian were: " Cerca di restare sotto lo sguardo di Dio, e Dio ti farà sempre da testimonio."

they were in a book, hopefully with many readers, how many people might not only become enlightened by some of these accounts, but, God willing, recipients of new graces such as have been granted to me and others fortunate enough to have known Padre Pio personally and to have been influenced by his help. The confirmation of which Padre Pio spoke.

I felt this urge to be an indication of a road to follow and could find no inner peace until I acted upon it. It has taken courage to attempt to put together a book of such a nature with my limited writing ability, but it would have taken more courage not to have done so; to refuse to be an instrument of bringing so much promised good to others. I was " backed-up " as the saying goes—the only thing asked of me was honesty, sincerity, and good will. The rest would remain between God and the reader.

And so dear reader, dear friend, if you can bear with my lack of literary ability, keeping your eye fixed rather on the deeper values that form the essence, I am certain, because of Padre Pio's words, that your perseverance will bear fruit.

*Awakening.*

Now, because of the natural sequence of things, I will have to begin with my story, of the road which led me to Padre Pio. Naturally, many things will not be told, and some barely touched upon. It is not easy to write of certain mystical experiences, and furthermore, it is a great responsibility, for it is in them, in a very particular way, that God manifests His enormous and individual love for each of us. His comprehension of our personality, limits and needs, is an invitation to go towards Him with confidence and, while these manifestations are often of an unbelievable simplicity, they are at the same time often deeply elusive and it is difficult for an inexperienced writer like myself not to shatter their fragile beauty. And yet I must go on. My hope is in simplicity. The one great message my overflowing heart has, at this moment, is: " If we really want to LIVE, we must abandon ourselves to our Creator."

All that is absolutely necessary is an " act of the will " on our part, simply saying, " God, my Father, direct me, guide me, protect me." If we are sincere, He will, in His way, and in His time, take care of the rest.

Sometimes, upon meeting a person who does not believe in the Divine Presence in our Church, or who claims to be an atheist, I can only suggest: " There are many intelligent persons who share your opinion, but remember that there are those, equally intelligent, who do not. Even though intelligent, you might be mistaken. If you really are sincere and of good-will, just put your foot inside a Catholic church and say: " Here I am .... This is the way I see things .... If you really exist and are here, and I am mistaken in my ideas, please enlighten me."

If there is no Divine Presence in the church, and no God above us in the heavens, what can one lose by such a simple act? Nothing! But, if one is mistaken, what can one find? Everything!

If something holds us back and keeps us from doing this, we will be able to face ourselves, perhaps for the first time, and realize that we are not sincere, and that it is not true that we do not believe. It might be more true that we are afraid of believing since it might obligate us to love our neighbor more fully; to become less egotistical; to give up a disorderly, dishonest or immoral way of life or an idea we have decided not to rid ourselves of. Even this enlightenment will be a great step forward.

I can remember years back, as I lay languidly on a sunny beach, saying to myself, " I have a terror of seeing a miracle because after such a manifestation one would feel obliged to give up many things and live a more active Christian life." Well, Our Divine Lord certainly took care of me, and now I will never find the words to thank Him.

I do not know exactly where to begin. Perhaps towards the end of World War II, would be a good starting point, because it was in one of those years that my act of the will took place.

Despite my good Catholic education, including a Catholic College degree, I cannot say I was a very good Catholic. Many things, such as pride, egoism, and an excessively material view of social problems blocked my horizon. I went to Mass on Sunday, received Holy Communion four or five times a year, and that was all. I never seemed to mature beyond this stage. The only prayers I said regularly were a certain number of Hail Marys each night for the repose of the souls of dear departed friends and relatives. (I was even a little doubtful about the existence of Purgatory but, just in case it did exist, I did not want to deny these persons at least a little help through my daily prayers.)

Not a very promising state of affairs. I do think I felt God deep down in me, but I wanted to reason too many things with my own head.

The basis, or beginning, of a new spiritual maturity in me was simply this: the war propaganda with its frequent distortion of reality. It so happened that I spent one war year in Italy, and the others in America. I was on the ocean on my way to the U. S. at the moment of the attack on Pearl Harbor and America's entry into the war.

During my year in Italy I read the exaggerations on one side and, during my war years in America, on the other side. A good part of the truth, and many of the mitigating circumstances were lost sight of and I was saddened. Gradually something was happening to me; a great submerged bell began to sound deep in my heart. I remembered my school years. I remembered the Gospel I had learned. Something told me with great certainty, " Only in the Gospel is the WHOLE TRUTH. This is the only printed word you can really completely believe in."

Although this conclusion bore no visible fruit for a long time, the root was very good—deep and strong—and something that was still in darkness began to move, to grow, to try to work itself toward the light.

Quite apart from the question of who was right or

who was wrong, I truly loved both countries, and had dear friends and relatives on both sides of the sea.

At this point, I must write something I would much prefer to omit, seeing how completely silly an act it was from a human point of view, though not displeasing to God who sees only the spirit and sincerity of our good will. I don't remember how I came upon it, but about this time a book containing several good spy stories fell into my hands. In its way it was colorful and well written, and while writing a letter to a Monsignor, a dear family friend, it seemed very natural to me to ask if one could not work in somewhat the same way for the Vatican.

I did not think of this as an act against any country. Quite the contrary! This could be a work that was, in some vague way, to benefit all, an impulsive need for connecting my whole-hearted enthusiasm with the new, deeper truth which had begun to stir deep down in me. But, at the same time, I was superficial and immature, still in search of color and adventure. All very childish, I know, even though in years I was far from being a child. I have since learned how many religious, social, and lay activities there are in the world, and how much good one can do if one wishes, but at that time I was ignorant of most of these opportunities.

Why am I writing of this? Because I am certain that God accepted my written offer, (a fact I did not realize for many years) and only upon looking back, am I able to see the design of things. A design that began to take definite form from that particular moment.

I was like one who signs up for the navy, is put on a ship and goes off to many ports, to many experiences, pleasant and otherwise. Returning to the port of embarkation after a long absence, he finally begins to understand what it means to be a sailor. I was " in service " though I did not yet know it, and I was to begin my spiritual journey under the greatest and most mysterious of directors!

Naturally, many ports, with their unexpected experiences, were touched upon which I will not speak of. I will go on to the sanctuary to which Divine Providence brought me when the waves were enormously high and tempestuous—the port of San Giovanni Rotondo. What I have just written, coupled with weeks of intense prayer, continuous supplication, and entreaty for Divine help is my proof that this was where God directed me and wanted me to find safety. Were I to deny San Giovanni Rotondo and Padre Pio, I would be denying God, His design, His wisdom and love, His answer to my prayers.

At the risk of causing the reader to smile cynically, I must now speak of a dream I had almost two years before I found myself in a most desperate spiritual dilemma.*

I never remember having had a dream of this type before, one which I felt sure was not just an ordinary dream, but one which came from some GREAT FORCE outside of me. In those first post-war years, there were

---

* At this point, I should tell the reader that I had returned to Italy after the war, supposedly for a few months, but the visit kept prolonging itself and a year or so later, I was joined by my mother and we found ourselves settling there more or less permanently among our friends and relatives.

not many automobiles in circulation, and so, in the afternoon, with my cousins and some friends, we frequently hiked up the main highway to a tiny, ancient church above Chiavari which bore the name " Madonna della Divine Grazie " -the same name, strangely enough, as the little Church sanctuary of San Giovanni Rotondo.

Not only was the little church near Chiavari old and lovely and of considerable artistic interest, but its elevated position dominating the entire Tigulian Gulf was magnificent, and we spent many a pleasant hour together chatting and enjoying the view. One night I dreamed I was on the road which led up to this little church. I was alone and very happy and seemed to be going up with great lightness and rapidity when, all at once, halfway up, the road became completely blocked by a great mass of rocks and stones. I attempted to climb over this obstacle but to no avail. It was too high and difficult. Disheartened, I had ceased my efforts when suddenly a great hand emerged from behind the rocks and, all at once, I found myself high up on the little square before the church, the obstacle having been mysteriously surmounted.

On this square there were three crosses—a Calvary— but I saw only the wooden base of each. I could not seem to raise my eyes because they were fixed on the horizon—a sea flooded with the most beautiful glimmering sunlight I had ever seen. My heart was filled with an ecstasy and joy that was not of this world.

I spoke of this dream very often with my cousins, and thought of it even more often. It gave me a great sense of hope, security, and a promised help of something wonderfully beautiful which lay ahead. And

36

so it was in great part, not only the remembrance of this dream, but my clinging faith in its promise of mysterious assistance that gave me the power to pray, to hope, and to keep open my dialogue with God and Our Lady whom I had just begun to discover and know. In the meantime, I will only say that I was suffering a great deal, completely tortured by a problem I just could not seem to resolve.

The strange part of this spiritual tension and heavy cross that I carried about with me all day was that, not only in the daytime was I able to go about my ordinary life in more or less the same way but, on going to bed at night, I could always sleep with tranquillity without the use of even a minimum sedative. I am absolutely certain that, humanly speaking, this was not possible. Only recently have I become conscious of this, and it is in part due to this conclusion that I felt the obligation of citing the letter and the offer written to my friend, the Monsignor. From that moment my life not only began to take on a strange new direction, but all along the way it was supported and kept in balance by some force outside of me. Without this mystic and yet positive help, I would have been engulfed in a sea of circumstances that my poor, frail human capacity alone could not have met and resolved. Each morning, upon awakening from my peaceful rest, there, waiting for me, was the heavy, dolorous cross which I realized had to be carried about all day. No one person could help me because no one person knew the whole truth. I felt trapped in a corner, and I prayed and prayed.

One morning, while at the beach, I confided a few

words of my anguished state of mind to a very sweet woman who was on a visit from Naples. " Why don't you go, or write to Padre Pio? ", she suggested. I really knew nothing about Padre Pio. Once or twice before, in happier moments, when someone had begun to speak of him, his stigmata, etc. I had stopped them immediately. " Fanaticism! " I would say, and that was that. Since then, the word " fanatic " produces a mixed emotion in me. In many cases the word is undoubtedly used correctly, but it is also one of the devil's favorite words, because it is connected with pride, making the user feel that he is more intelligent and superior to the so-called fanatic, and we know that pride is always to some degree, a blinding element.

" My sister," continued the woman, " is a spiritual daughter of his." (I wondered vaguely what " spiritual daughter " meant.) " She goes to him in moments of need and has always been helped. During the war, her son who was in the army had been missing for two years and she did not know whether he was dead or alive. Finally, she went to Padre Pio and after confession, confided her sorrow to him. ' Do not worry.' he said, ' your son is alive and well and will return soon to you in good health.' And so it happened. After a few months he did return home. Sometime later, her younger son, a boy of about twelve, became ill, swollen and he lost the power of speech. After examinations by a number of specialists who wanted to operate on his brain, she decided to take him to Bologna to a famous doctor there. However, she first brought him to Padre Pio to be blessed. Padre Pio consoled her saying, ' Do not worry, the boy does not have what the doctors think he has, and he needs no operation. A long cure will restore his health and speech.' Imagine her surprise when the doctor in Bologna repeated Padre Pio's words. After a long series of treatments it happened as both Padre Pio and the doctor said, and the boy spoke again."

## Letters and Replies

I was astounded and pleased to hear these accounts for it made me understand that here was a person who had powers beyond the human, a man of God and of mercy. She gave me his address and I hurried off to write, thinking he would personally answer me with a long letter. I did not know how many letters he received daily, nor that it was almost impossible for him to use a pen to any extent due to the wounds in his hands. His correspondence was all handled, then as now, by secretaries, and at that time the principal secretary was Dr. Sanguinetti, who also had begun and supervised the building of the hospital for Padre Pio.

In my letter, I merely stated, briefly, a part of my problem, feeling certain that with the powers he possessed he would understand everything. I concluded by saying: " Chiedo una Sua preghiera ed una parola di luce." (" I am asking for your prayers and a word of enlightenment.") Then I waited for my answer.

One night, three days after having mailed my letter, before putting out the light, I wound the little clock on my night table and remember very distinctly seeing that it was twelve-thirty. I settled down but despite my sleepiness I became more and more aware of a very heavy perfume of roses. I could not understand where it was coming from as I knew there were no flowers in my room and I used no perfume. Also, there were no roses in the garden four stories below. I lay there sleepily puzzled, not knowing how to find an explanation for the perfume and I remember stretching out my arm to reach underneath my bed to see if someone had hidden a bunch of roses there. Baffled, I finally fell asleep still breathing this delicious and mysterious perfume.

In the morning, I hurried off to the beach as usual and my mind did not for the moment return to the happening of the night before. On returning late, I found my father, a doctor, and my uncle, a lawyer, lingering over their meal. As I sat down hurriedly my uncle said, " I was just telling your father of the strangest thing that happened to me last night. Between twelve-thirty and one o'clock I was sitting in bed reading a book when all at once a perfume of fresh flowers passed under my nose and then left. I was very surprised and wondered if it was a mysterious announcement of a death or funeral, but then I realized it was not. It was too fresh, light and pleasant a fragrance. When it disappeared, it was followed one by one by the perfume of four different fresh flowers—first gardenia, then carnation, violet, and then . . . !

Well, nothing like this ever happened to me before! I just cannot understand it."

Upon hearing this, I suddenly remembered the perfume of roses the night before. " Why, do you know, now that you speak of this, I too, at the same time, noticed a strong perfume of roses in my room. What does all this mean? " We looked at one another wonderingly.

I had never heard anyone speak of Padre Pio and his " perfumes," and so did not even remotely connect any of these manifestations with the letter I had written, and as far as my uncle was concerned, he was completely ignorant of the fact that I had even written, so I do not think anyone could accuse either of us of autosuggestion.

While we were talking about all these things, our dear old family maid who was serving lunch, listened attentively. She was the only one in the house who knew I had written to Padre Pio since I had given her the letter to mail. Upon retiring to my room after the meal, she entered suddenly. " Signorina, when I was in the kitchen something seemed to say in my ear: it is Padre Pio who has answered the Signorina's letter! " I don't remember for certain, but I am afraid I lost patience at hearing her words. " Andreina, what can perfumes have to do with my letter or the answer to it? " However, I became even more puzzled. Later, about four o'clock, upon going out, I encountered a friend who, when I recounted what had happened, explained about Padre Pio and his perfumes, and that this meant his nearness, his answer, his prayers, and that the perfume of roses was a very good sign, usually meaning that the grace one asked would be given. Hope and joy and a smile that might almost be classified as a giggle began to mix themselves within the torment in my heart. Hope, because I saw that I was understood, and that this mysterious force knew much more of my problem than I had revealed in my letter, and a giggle because of the humorous way it had manifested this understanding to me. Because, had the perfume come only to me, upon speaking of it, I would certainly have been told that my imagination was running away with me. The reality of the perfume which had been sent to me was confirmed and protected by the perfumes which had been sent to my uncle. Also, he had spoken of them first! I felt I had an invisible but present friend who walked with me and accompanied me, almost hand in hand, a friend who was a great artist, and who " bore witness."

With great confidence, I wrote my second letter, this time including an offering for the church. I thanked him for the perfumes, assuring him of my faith in him, his prayers, etc., and ended by repeating that I was still waiting for his written answer with its words of enlightenment. Two days later, in full daylight, while putting on my sandals, an extremely strong perfume of lillies was wafted under my nose. It was intense, but unlike the perfume of roses, did not last or hover over me, and disappeared almost in a flash as it had come. And so I knew the second letter had been received and again I admired the technique of making me believe in the truth and reality of the perfume's appearance and message. The first one had come at night in a heavy, soft wave and lingered and was of roses. Certainly, I was not expecting lillies in full daylight while holding an old shoe in my hand, and with such force and rapidity.

Again my sense of humor was tickled and my inward state of sadness comforted with a smile. Again that wonderful feeling of not walking alone, and of being understood.

Once more I took my pen in hand to write words of thanks and faith, assuring Padre Pio that I would believe and follow the counsel given in the letter I was awaiting—that word of " light " which I expected. Again I sent an offering.

Then my long wait began. No more perfumes came and no letter arrived. Every morning I would hurry down to the post office to wait for our mailman to emerge, to ask him if I had any mail. No love letter was ever more anxiously awaited. One week passed, then a second and a third. They seemed eternal. I kept praying and waiting, praying and waiting. The anguished feeling had returned. I began to feel confused and abandoned. I just could not understand what was happening, but throughout this strange interval, this silence, this moment of trial, I did pray insistently, always clinging to my faith in the promised help of my dream and remembering the perfumed answers to my letters.

About this time, during a discussion about dreams among our group at the beach, a young psychiatrist from Milan said that dreams come only from within ourselves, psychic conditions, etc. And so I began to dialogue with God, to ask Him about the answer to this question. I spoke to Him as a child might ask an earthly father about another order of things. I asked about that dream; was I mistaken in believing that a dream could come from Him, from a force outside of me? God answered in His own mystic way.

Our apartment was on a high fourth floor, and from my terraced window, I had a wonderful view of the Mediterranean and the point of Portofino. In the morning it was in perfect light and, as I sipped my cup of coffee in bed before arising, I drank and drank of that beauty. One day workers suddenly appeared in the street below and began to move busily about. After much to-do, an iron, high tension electrical pole arose, disfiguring the residential area, and rearing its ugly length between me and my view. An artistic disaster! I was very saddened by this but don't believe I spoke of it to anyone because of its short duration for, after a morning or two, upon opening the shutters, my heart leaped with joy. The same laborers were dismantling their previous work and my view was unblocked and there was the horizon, the sea and Portofino!

With a lighter and happier heart I went off to the beach where the usual cluster of cousins and friends were grouped under the usual umbrellas. A young married chap of about twenty-eight by the name of Piero Solari who had a degree in agriculture, upon seeing me arrive, got up and came and sat down under the umbrella next to me. " Clarice," he said, " I must tell you of the strangest dream I had of you last night. I dreamed I saw you sitting on top of one of those big high-tension electrical poles and, as I passed below, you called me and said happily, " Piero, Piero, come up. I have re-found my view of Portofino." I looked at him stupefied. It was one of the few times in my life words failed me.

We spoke of the strangeness of this dream for days, for he had known nothing of the existence of the short-lived pole, much less of its dismantling, and absolutely nothing of my emotions regarding the whole procedure since both of us were positive I had never opened my mouth regarding the subject.

Certainly no one could say this dream came from within him, and so I understood that God had answered the sincerity of my request with the simplicity and perfect art of which only He is capable. Our loving Father is always so near to us, and I felt as though He were explaining in His fatherly, patient way: " You see, my dear, dreams can come from within your head or even from indigestion, but when I WANT, they can also come from outside of you."

And so, more and more, I began to live in another world and to cling with greater and greater faith to the promise of that dream, of that wonderful hand, that symbolic hand. Yet I walked with the same anguished feeling, and every morning I hurried off to the post office in hopeful expectation though still no letter arrived. It was really very baffling!

I remember lying on my bed one afternoon with my hands joined in prayer, feeling as though my strength were at an end, as though I could not endure this state of things much longer. Despite this, however, that very morning I remember writing in a letter: " Ma io credo nella Divina Provvidenza, butto una Salve Regina dopo l'altra al cielo, e un giorno o l'altro, non potrà resistere e quella porta dovrà aprirsi." (But I believe in Divine Providence, and I am literally hurling one " Hail, Holy Queen! " after another towards heaven, and one day or another it will no longer be able to resist, and that door will have to open.)

At this point, I must pause to make clear that I had never heard anyone speak of Padre Pio's power of bilocation.

That night, after going to bed, my darkened room became flooded with a strange illumination like moonlight, and there, seated at the foot of my bed on one of my small, upholstered armchairs was a monk who, because of his half-gloved hands, I intuitively understood was Padre Pio. There was nothing dramatic or solemn about all this, his attitude was completely natural—like that of a friend who had come to call, to visit. One hand was resting half inserted in the rope (cordone) around his waist. I was frightened and I wasn't frightened. Very calmly he said three words to me, but I did not understand them. I tried to light the lamp next to my bed and, although I pushed the button conected to the switch, nothing happened. Again, very calmly, he repeated three words which again I did not understand and again I tried to light the lamp without success. And a third time, the same thing, another three words which I did not understand and the light switch that did not function. Suddenly the moonlight and Padre Pio vanished. I saw only my darkened room, and upon touching the light, my little lamp functioned perfectly just in time for me to see my bedroom door open by itself as if someone were leaving! Something in my heart seemed to whisper: The Three words of light (enlightenment) are " The door will open! " (Le tre parole di luce sono: LA PORTA S'APRIRÀ.)

Three times he had pronounced three words making nine. In this phrase in Italian there are nine words! Then, as almost always, the confirmation outside of myself—the closed door opening completely in full light before my eyes. The answer to my letter of that morning. Divine Providence—THE DOOR HAD OPENED!

I sat, I don't know how long, looking at that open door which in the silent and windless night had opened completely. I felt certain, now more than ever, of that help, and my faith grew stronger. I no longer waited so desperately for the material letter of reply. I felt that something was taking care of me, taking care of working out everything for me, and I was almost happy that no real letter ever arrived. (Nor did one ever arrive, despite the three letters I had written, two of which contained offerings.)

I was still obsessed with my problem and the way to resolve it, difficult because of its spiritual side—the part, that is, which involved my conscience. Although still suffering, I was distracted, and began falling in love with this, my new world, that more and more possessed my thoughts. It was as though gradually the material world was becoming immaterial, and the immaterial world concrete. They were changing place from the way they had presented themselves before my purely human eyes.

I remember closing the shutters of my french doors before retiring one night and, standing on the terrace for a moment gazing at the bright lights of Portofino and the Riviera scintillating in the summer night, symbolic of the world and its gaiety, and the best and worst the world has to offer in the way of diversion, smiling to myself, I remember thinking " you simply don't interest me any more." They could not stand up under the competition of the master hand of another Artist—the

Artist who was the essence of truth and love who, with a few brief strokes of pen or brush, so to speak, could say so much, whose art made one live!

I was lost in admiration, and in love—in love much more perhaps than I even realized. The strange part of all this was that no thought of going to Padre Pio passed through my mind until, in October, my mother and I went down to Rome to visit our dear friend, Margherita Hamilton, and she suggested that, after all my experiences, I go to San Giovanni Rotondo and to confession to Padre Pio. She, too, was anxious to go, never having been there. I resisted a good deal before acquiescing, feeling as though, after all these happenings, it was almost a lack of faith in the promised help. Satan uses all methods to keep us far from that holy mountain, the tiny church of Our Lady of Divine Grace and Padre Pio. Finally, after not only thinking about it but asking spiritual advice as well, I decided in the affirmative and, leaving my mother comfortably settled in Rome, the two of us took off on our great adventure. Both of us seemed filled with the same sense of joy and anticipation.

The only good fast train, at that time, left at midnight from Rome and was very crowded, to say the least. Yet we were able to pass the whole night alone in a compartment by ourselves, each of us stretched out comfortably on the three seats on either side. No one disturbed us. The crisp October night was laden with stars, shooting stars, falling stars.

The extremely fast Rapido flew on its way to Foggia, to San Giovanni Rotondo, and to Padre Pio. We had both done a bit of traveling and Daisy (as we familiarly called her) had even spent some months in India, but no trip was ever like this one. Our hearts were filled with a strange, indescribable joy. " Just think," murmured Daisy, " I even have friends in Rome who belong to the highest nobility, who come to Padre Pio on pilgrimages of prayer, and who, for penance, buy a third-class ticket and sit up all night on the hard wooden seats." This seemed, at the moment, the height of all imaginable penances. Neither of us imagined how often this was to happen in our lives ... particularly in mine!

But, although the soft couches of that night, the spectacular sky with its profusion of stars, and the vibrant happiness that possessed us, were never again repeated in quite the same way, yet that happiness has transformed itself into a more profound joy which has remained and has grown. Joy that no hard wooden seat or series of sleepy and tired arrivals in the cold, gray dawn at the station in Foggia could ever lessen or obliterate.

*Arrival at San Giovanni Rotondo.*

That morning, after a bit of confusion due to many unusual circumstances, we finally found and boarded our bus for San Giovanni Rotondo, forty miles distant and, once settled, started the last leg of our adventurous journey, passing through the war ruins of many demolished buildings in this heavily bombed city. Gradually, we emerged and found ourselves in the country, at first barren and flat, and later tortuously hilly, as we began the six hundred meter climb which was to take us up to San Giovanni Rotondo.

Everywhere, one had a sense of limitless horizons, as limitless as the immensity of graces Our Lord dispensed in such abundance from this poor, unknown village, this humble sanctuary, this tiny confessional. The countryside was of rocky formation, gray and irregular, interspersed here and there with numerous olive and almond trees, the characteristic agricultural cultivation of this locality. The primitive village of San Giovanni Rotondo had to be traversed before arriving at the convent and sanctuary of Santa Maria delle Grazie, the two being separated by a distance of another two miles.

Now, especially since the construction of Padre Pio's great hospital—the Casa Sollievo della Sofferenza—this village has made progress and has become somewhat modernized, although still very modest, but at that time, it was truly poor and one encountered many men and women in their typical local dress, mounted on mules, along the road. In the central part of town, one could see housewives going to the well with urns to draw water for their household necessities, there being no running water in many buildings.

Everything represented a truly new world, different, at least for me, from any hitherto known. We established ourselves in what was at the time the newest and best hotel. I will only say that it was fairly clean and in order, even though certainly not very comfortable, and, because of its newness, still quite damp. We would have continued to stay there however, had it not been so far down the road from the convent and the little church of Santa Maria delle Grazie where Padre Pio celebrated the Holy Sacrifice of the Mass at five o'clock each morning. And so, deciding that a walk of more than a mile uphill at four o'clock was a little too much, the next day we moved up to a small villa right under the convent where a few rooms were rented only to those who had a letter of introduction, as Daisy had.

*The Church and Our Pensione.*

Of the first hours, I remember very little, because at that time there were no afternoon services of any kind. After about ten in the morning all activity was suspended until the five o'clock Mass on the following morning. After Mass, Padre Pio heard the confessions of about thirty women; distributed Holy Communion to a hundred or more persons, and then terminated his visible activities at Santa Maria delle Grazie. I only remember, and scarcely know how to describe, the emotion—the strangeness of entering this small church for the first time, so Franciscan in its child-like simplicity, so heart-warming and cordial, almost like a

51

heavenly hearth fallen upon this earth with our dear Mother Mary, for hostess, smilling so tenderly, and waiting, it seemed, for each one of us. In her arms, that little Babe, so like and so unlike all others—her real offering to us.

In one angle, the confessional of Padre Pio—the spiritual bath for the tired pilgrim come so far, laden with the burden of his dusty sins and worldly sorrows and preoccupations. I looked long at that empty confessional where my mystic " friend " spent hours each day. I seemed to feel his nearness and yet could not realize, in a way, that he truly, materially existed, and that I was so close to him. Over the main altar-railing was an arch, its inside curve painted naively with a floral design of roses and lillies. My two perfumes! I felt a little like the child of my fairy-book days—and yet so terribly different.

How many truths and worlds I was to discover in that humble little church. How many universes and horizons enclosed within the small space of those walls!

On the right-hand side of the church, facing Padre Pio's confessional, under three low vaults, were three small altars all in a row and quite close to one another. The first one, upon entering the church was dedicated to St. Anthony with the same quaint statue posted above it that one sees in any of the more modest type Catholic churches all over the world—the faraway smile, the infant in his arms. The middle one contained a large painting of an apparition of Our Lady. The last one, closest to the main altar, was dedicated to St. Francis of Assisi, with the statue enclosed in a glassed-in niche. It was at this altar that Padre Pio for many years offered his pre-dawn Mass. This one, as the other two, was encircled by a wooden elevation of no more than one step in height so that the celebrant was raised but very little above the surrounding congregation. This made visibility difficult, as the priest was easily obstructed by the closely packed heads of the people grouped tightly about in circular standing position, necessitated by the limited size of the miniature church. It was for this reason that everyone struggled to get in first in the morning, when the wee door of the wee church was opened by a rather frightened monk, shortly before five o'clock. This scene was to make our debut a breathless and unexpected experience; a whirlwind, let us call it, with the result that between being literally hurled inside in this manner, combined with our rather stunned tiredness and ignorance of the whole routine, (we still thought, that first morning, that the Holy Mass would take place at the large center altar), we went to the opposite side up front, and took our place in one of the few ordinary pews facing the main altar. Between the crowd, the distance that divided us, and the two rather squat, fat pillars upholding the three altar vaults, we scarcely had a glimpse of Padre Pio. But, perhaps this was just as well. We were content to be enclosed in the same little intimate church with him. We felt his spiritual nearness, his nearness mixed with God's nearness, all fused in some wonderful mystery. We felt we were " in port! "

Yes, I think everything was as it was meant to be. Outside the stars were still visible, still flickering. In some remote place was the world—trains, noise, large cities, movement. Here was nothing and everything—hushed silence, peace, repose and prayer.

After my pre-San Giovanni Rotondo experience, this surely was the right beginning, for we were thus introduced to this whole new atmosphere gradually. The clear view of the entire Mass would perhaps have been too much all at once. Everything, as always, artistically worked out—a blending one might almost say, not a sudden shock. And then, too, perhaps it was designed that my first clear view of Padre Pio should be in his open confessional, sitting with his hand half in his cord, just as I had seen him in my room in Chiavari, that strange night—to meet his eyes directly, those same sweetly severe eyes that calmly and penetratingly took one in at a glance, and seemed to say: " So you are here! "

The little house under the church, in its nest of almond trees, where we succeeded in renting two rooms, was to be another of the vivid, never-to-be-forgotten memories of our first trips to San Giovanni Rotondo, and very particularly of the initial one. A very dear woman, Signora Maria, already past middle age, had built it for her own use, thinking, I believe, very little of renting rooms, but because of its proximity to the church, pilgrim after pilgrim came knocking at her door. And so, for charity's sake, she had put up two or three cots in an English basement's few rooms. Later, by degrees, she would add a new wing and another floor above.* The moment of our arrival was, however, the bare beginning

* I am speaking of conditions about 1951. Now everything has improved. There are modern quarters and hotels with rooms and bath.

of this transition and building. There were, of course, no meals served. The first floor had four rooms, one an entrance and living room combined which contained a cot or daybed. Another was Signora Maria's bedroom and next to it was a smaller but warm room with a sunny exposure and a fairly normal bed which she reserved for a niece during her visits. This room was given to Daisy. The remaining one, a cold corner room with northern exposure and damp walls, which one could scarcely call furnished, was given to me. The damp condition also was due to the newness of the construction. There was a wooden chair and a night stand, consisting of a piece of wood placed upon two rows of bricks for legs. I am not certain, but I think that the only table in the room was also at least partly upheld by bricks. My impression of that room was of bricks, bricks, bricks— and great spots of dampness on the ceiling and walls. But, the prize piece of furniture in the room was the bed—that unforgetable bed! Never in the wildest flights of imagination could I ever have thought of having to sleep on a similar object. I don't remember upon what the mattress rested, but I do remember that rest I did not! It was perhaps half a yard shorter than average length, and much narrower than normal, and it was stuffed with dried leaves and corn husks. Fortunately, at the time I was rather slender. The only note of hope in the entire room (which made me prefer it to going down to the mysterious basement and separating myself from Daisy,) was a wood-burning stove in the corner which dear Signora Maria assured me could be lighted in the evening to help ward off the cold humidity. Little did we know that at San Giovanni Rotondo, particularly at that time, things just happened in their own good time and way (the beginning of our school of patience!) and so naturally it took at least twenty-four hours before a bit of wood made its appearance and another twenty-four to discover that the stove did not draw, and still another twenty-four to think of whom to call to fix it, after which one just had to wait for this individual to arrive and go to work and produce the miracle of a flame from those few sticks.

In the afternoon Daisy would take cover in her bed and doze or read but I, despite my tiredness, having no place even to sit comfortably, took to walking sleepily up and down the road to keep warm. In this way, I found my steps leading toward the little church where the much-needed cleaning hour was in progress. Two or three of the local women volunteered to do this work and occasionally some pilgrim like myself wandered in and lent a hand. I wandered in, but the hand I lent did not meet with very much approval. I shall never forget the scolding I received for taking a broom and beginning to sweep the dusty old tiles, without the use of the damp sawdust which the others were employing in this chore. Gradually, I became more expert and more attached to this activity because of my great personal affection for this little church which seemed like a home—the home of homes! I felt the work to be an honor and privelege, and on each subsequent visit to San Giovanni Rotondo, brought all the novelties that could be found in the line of cleaning equipment to the now friendly and affectionate " Annunziata " of San Giovanni Rotondo who presented herself with great fidelity and perspiration almost daily, saying: " Keeps me out of temptation," as vigorously she moved pews and benches.

More and more I learned to love each inch of the little altars and broken-down confessionals; the wondrous and always new glimpses of sky, clouds, cypress and pine trees, visible from the two tiny windows on high. This strange little church had so many ways of entering into your heart and of thanking you for your work. What poetry I really lived in those days.

Over the entrance, facing the main altar, was a sort of choir loft—only it wasn't used for this purpose. It was a place of prayer where the monks not only meditated and prayed, but also recited their office. Sometimes we arrived in time to hear a bit of these half-chants and we would work in silence, trying to discern which was Padre Pio's voice—almost always discernible because of its velvety, fullthroated cadence. In all his prayers there seemed to be a tear, and despite his dynamic life and, at times, briefness of words spoken in his confessional, I don't remember ever hearing him hurry one single word of a prayer. He said each one whole-heartedly, as though it were completely new and recited in the Divine Presence.

In the center of the railing of this loft was a huge crucifix which had its back to the church below. Painted on the ceiling directly above the crucifix was a fresco of St. Michael the Archangel, the figure that was repeated under that of Our Lady of Divine Grace in the center of the main altar. It was in this loft and before this crucifix that Padre Pio received his stigmata years ago and was found bleeding and unconscious by his brother monks.

And so, after the Divine Presence that was everywhere, and Our Lady of Divine Grace in her predominant position above the tabernacle of the main altar, the three saintly figures remembered in the little church were, as I have already said, St. Francis of Assisi, St. Anthony of Padua, and last, but not least, St. Michael the Archangel, whose grotto church was not many miles away. I hope to speak more of him, and the angelical world in general for he, too, is one of the great inspirations which induced me to take my pen in hand. Among all these, Padre Pio, the most mystic and the most human of friends who seemed to have a foot in each of these two worlds, a " trait d'union," uniting and fusing them. In him, the strong vibration of God's divine love for us was mixed with humility, simplicity and a human, fraternal, warm-heartedness—a true wearer of the Franciscan habit with its nothing and its all. He, the human go-between who, with all his sufferings had pledged himself as a sacrifice in his tremendous love of God and of his fellow man, to console, comfort, and most important of all, to enlighten spiritually, all who came, by the grace of God, into the realm of his awareness. Impossible not to fear him, impossible not to love him, impossible not to feel how much above one he was—his immense PATERNITY.

And now, let us return to the little villa. Our genteel hostess was not lacking in charity in providing me with such, let us say, disagreeable quarters. She was not of San Giovanni Rotondo and had established herself there only because of Padre Pio. She had built the small villa for her own use, without the project of renting rooms and, therefore, the house was not designed for this purpose, and the odd, incomplete room given me was never rented to anyone. It was used only by a night watchman who dropped by for a few hours now and then. As a matter of fact, at the time we pounced in on her, she was in the act of tearing up letters and ridding herself of many personal belongings in order, in the not too distant future, to leave her nice, large, corner room, with its sunny terrace, for pilgrims like us. She would soon transfer herself to a little room in the half-basement, half-ground-floor (the ground was irregular) from which modest room she never again moved until her rather recent death. She was a truly Franciscan soul and I would not want the smallest shadow to fall on her memory! Perhaps, since hers was the house closest to the convent and Padre Pio, it was not meant to be too comfortable. After a certain length of time we did get the stove to draw a little, and in the evenings, we lit it for awhile which did help things out.

In the meantime, however, it is undeniable that the hours spent in that room were rather a torture. Only with the help of my extreme fatigue and the hot water bottle which my hostess so thoughtfully placed upon the crackly mattress, was I able to fall into a profound sleep for a few hours. Then, awakening, I would shiver and shake in the dampness until the four o'clock rising hour. Only in the warm little church would I gradually thaw out and come back to normal.

It so happened that, in one of these early morning hours, I awakened feeling very badly indeed. I was feverish and wheezed when I breathed. It was evident that my condition was serious enough to require a long stay in bed, a fact which caused me to despair. How was I ever going to stay in that bed for days? An utter impossibility! As these thoughts were going through my mind, I became aware of a strong aroma of something like eucalyptus, and then another different smell of ointment. The eucalyptus I understood immediately was in some way connected with Padre Pio's perfume world, but the ointment odor which seemed to emerge from the blankets, filled me with disgust. I wondered who had used that bedding before me, and even the eucalyptus made me sad as it was too much of a change after the delicious perfumes of roses and lillies. I could not understand its significance, except perhaps as some sort of reproval. However, shortly afterwards, I fell into a deep sleep and when the four o'clock alarm rang for Mass, far from staying in bed I got up and, hastily and sleepily, jumped into my clothes and raincoat, tied my usual woolen babushka about my head, and went and stood on the threshold of Daisy's room while she dressed. " Daisy," I said sleepily, " I am terribly sick." As I said these words, the strong smell of the ointment returned to my nostrils. Daisy says she will never forget the look of surprise on my face. " Oh!," I said, " Then that smell was not in the bed! " The odor seemed to say, " How stupid you are. Don't you realize it was all medicinal? " I breathed deeply and did not wheeze. " Daisy," I said, " I am well. There's nothing wrong with me! "

Completely bewildered, and full of marvel, I stood with Daisy a few minutes later on the piazetta before the church with the other pilgrims, waiting for the church door to be opened for Sunday Mass. I just could not seem to grasp what had happened, and felt an overwhelming need to speak of it to someone. Next to us were two men, one of whom I later discovered was Carlo Trabucco, now an editorial writer for the Catholic weekly magazine " Orizzonti " but, at that time, I believe, a sports writer for a daily newspaper. He had first met Padre Pio when he had come to San Giovanni Rotondo to interview a young woman, a well-known communist, who had died at San Giovanni Rotondo after being converted by Padre Pio. His own encounter with Padre Pio had been a rather dramatic one, almost a conversion, for he subsequently admitted in one of his articles that Padre Pio had, figuratively speaking, " pulled the rug from under his feet " by a remark at their first meeting.

At that moment, I did not know who he was. I knew only that he had slept on the daybed in our entrance, a bed which was reserved for him on his brief, but fairly numerous visits to San Giovanni Rotondo. He was large, husky, sportily dressed, and wore a beret. After a few remarks back and forth, I could not contain myself and blurted out what had just happened, thinking it would produce heaven only knows what sort of a reaction, but nothing of the sort! At home such a tale would have provoked at best a tongue in cheek attitude and perhaps an ironical smile. Instead, here were two healthy, intelligent men who did not blink an eye, nor did they doubt any of my words. I gathered from their remarks that the smell of eucalyptus was not new to them, but the ointment odor was, and they were calmly discussing this when the church door opened and, in the confusion of entering, we lost sight of one another.

Dear reader, all I can say is that it is one thing to

sit here calmly writing these things and for you to read them, but it is quite another to have passed through the emotion of experiencing them, just an hour or two before, to find oneself suddenly " in port " in the crowded little church with the first signs of dawn just becoming visible from the slits of windows, there in the warm candlelight of the little altar of St. Francis of Assisi, to see Padre Pio arrive, his stigmatized hands joined in prayer, his face pallid, his great eyes fixed with such humble, immense love as he gazed at the crucifix, to see him mount the altar step, quietly signing himself with the sign of the cross, and begin to offer the Mass.

I was filled with awe and love, fear and mystery and, again, that sense of the whirling world outside being farther and farther away; of being less and less important; of everything most wonderful being enclosed here; and, in my heart—gratitude, gratitude!

*Cigarettes.*

I don't remember at this moment if a certain decision of mine was made before or during this visit to San Giovanni Rotondo, but I do remember confiding it to Daisy, and her never-forgotten words of counsel—and she a convert! One of my greatest hopes would be that these words of her's could encircle the world, and that everyone, upon reading them, would let them penetrate deeply and put them into practice.

"«Daisy," I said, " if I obtain the grace I have come here to ask of Padre Pio, I have promised to give up smoking, since that is the thing that would cost me the most sacrifice, and to send the more or less five thousand lire of cigarette money each month to Padre Pio for his hospital." " Non commerciare con Dio," she said. " DON'T BARGAIN WITH GOD." " Hai da fare con un grande Signore! " " YOU ARE DEALING WITH A GREAT LORD. HE WILL TAKE CARE OF THE REST." These words pierced me like an arrow and, for the gift of them, I shall always be tied to her by an unyielding knot, for we can never really rid our " spiritual » hearts of words of light, nor of their donor, and also, because putting these words into practice has poured upon me such a constant rainfall of graces and abundance of Divine help and enlightenment in every sense, as to render me eternally in her debt.

" Very well, I will give them up before asking or obtaining this grace for which I came to San Giovanni Rotondo. However, it will have to be done by degrees." And so began my struggle. For a few days all went fairly well, and I was rather pleased with myself, thinking I was going to make it and arrive at my goal, having reduced my original eighteen cigarettes to about six a day and not smoking the first one until eleven in the morning.

However, due to the hardships, fatigue and tension of the unusual life we were leading under such rugged circumstances, it proved more than difficult. And so, about eight o'clock one morning, in my brick laden room, I just felt I could not carry on without a cigarette so I lit my first one almost three hours ahead of time. After the first satisfying puffs, my little traveling clock began glaring at me with disapproval and I was smitten with a terrible sadness, feeling that I was back at the starting point and not making any progress—that I simply was not going to make the grade. The spirit was willing, but the flesh was weak! Overwhelmed by a great wave of discouragement and sadness, I began to cry, and putting the burning cigarette in the lone ashtray on the table I went to the suitcase to get a handkerchief to dry my tears. Upon returning to the table and to my cigarette, I found an empty ashtray. Very annoyed, I began looking for the cigarette. Where in the world could it have fallen? Between the wooden table, the sticks for the stove and above all, my mattress, the room was a veritable unlighted bonfire. Hurriedly and fearfully, I began searching for it, becoming constantly more alarmed. Daisy's help was implored before flames should emerge from some unexpected corner. Together we went to work but to no avail. I became more and more apprehensive and, finding the fifteen year old maid, put her to work also. We looked everywhere—bed, suitcase, every spot on and around the table. We were three hectic women in a topsy-turvy room. While all this was going on, a poor, rather bedraggled man arrived from nowhere and stood on the threshold watching us. We were so intent in our search that we scarcely noticed him. It did not, at that particular time, seem unnatural that he should be standing there. Finally, in the same moment that an exasperated impatience took possession of me, there dawned a vague, but strong suspicion that something unnatural had taken place—that some sort of a trick had been played on me and the mere thought that there might be a recurrence

*iew of the little Sanctuary (1952) and moments of
adre Pio's Mass.*

of this was too much for me to bear. On the table against the wall, stacked one package on top of another, was my provision of cigarettes—vermillion packages of Macedonia d'oro Extra. Grasping them, and suddenly becoming aware of the poor working man standing in the doorway, I thrust them all into his hands. He accepted them eagerly and left immediately. Where he went no one knows, just as none of us ever discovered where he came from. But, the very important part of this story is that, not only have I never, in the eighteen years past, put a cigarette to my lips, but from that moment I CEASED TO DESIRE THEM! I can remember saying to Daisy that day, " Daisy, two hours have passed and I haven't smoked and I don't care. Daisy, five hours have passed and I have no desire for a cigarette. I don't even remember what one tastes like. Looking at a cigarette or looking at a stone produces the same reaction."

*More of Padre Pio*

The following morning at Mass, a new aspect of Padre Pio began to emerge and to make me wonder if perhaps he was not carrying some of the cross I had been too weak to bear. The thought, the revelation of the burden of suffering he offered to assume for the needy and anguished who came to implore graces through his intercession, plunged down and touched my heart in a depth never before reached by any other creature, and although I had learned to pray and dialogue with God because of my tormenting situation, yer I still had to learn another solitary form of formal prayer, such as saying the rosary alone, which had always seemed an interminable procedure to me. Suddenly, I found myself kneeling on the cold, hard, tiled floor of the little church with my rosary and, without moving, for the first time in my life, recited four rosaries in a row, imploring Almighty God to be merciful and not to let Padre Pio suffer too much for us, but rather to lighten his cross.

From that moment, I began to feel lonesome without a rosary in my hand—my anchor of safety! This new joy, this gift of prayer, began to grow from that instant and thus began my almost daily recital of the rosary for Padre Pio's intentions and sufferings—a gift sent by the Good Lord who never lets Himself be outdone in generosity.

The hour of the Holy Sacrifice of the Mass celebrated by Padre Pio also began to present itself in a new light, with two completely contradictory sides. Perhaps here was the great force of it all. One part complemented the other. On the one hand, the human, intimate, warm side—all of us grouped like children so closely about the little candlelit altar of St. Francis. So much more human, it seemed, than Masses said in other churches! On the other hand, the sense of the immense spiritual distance which separated us from Padre Pio the mystic, so mysteriously and completely above us. His great nearness and intimacy with God. Their conversing together. He seemed to walk his earthly way like Our Lord. A union of all that was most human, with all that was most divine.

After the morning Mass which ended about six-thirty, we hurried back to our pensione and slipped back into bed for a while. Daisy rested, and I did the best I could. Then we returned to church to be present for the women's confession period which lasted between an hour and a half to two hours. When the confession period was finished, Padre Pio distributed Holy Communion from the main altar until perhaps nine-thirty. Due to the numerous communicants, and because of his painful, stigmatized feet, instead of his going to the altar railing and having to walk a great deal back an forth, each communicant passed through the altar railing gate and knelt, in groups of seven or eight, at the top of the three interval altar steps closest to the altar iself. In this way, Padre Pio was saved much useless movement. This, of course, brought the recipient in to much closer contact with him than in the normal procedure where the altar railing serves as a division.

Daisy and I did not, on this first trip, receive Holy Communion until after our confession with him. It seemed the prize of our penance filled journey—communion received in wonderful certainty that one was truly clean and absolved, and without any doubt in the state of grace. Later, we became more enlightened and went up, already confessed and prepared for our daily communion which, as time went on became more than a habit—it became a necessity in our everyday lives.

These three spiritual activities of Padre Pio's (that is, Mass, confession and the distribution of Holy Communion), represented or made visible three aspects of his many-sided, rich personality. In the Holy Sacrifice of the Mass, the mystic, his prayers, his tears, his long pauses in ecstasy, his almost intimate conversation with the Host he held in his hand—an appointment of love with God, the Infinite and Divine.

Later, in giving the Host to us, one again saw the mystic, whose whole expression changed the moment he took the Holy Eucharist in hand, but mixed with a paternal attitude as he bent over each one of us, never showing for one instant a sign of hurry, of suffering, or fatigue, but only profound joy and satisfaction in being able to give to us that which he knew to be the most precious of gifts—the greatest source of light and strength, our spiritual daily bread referred to in the Lord's Prayer.

In the confessional period which preceded this distribution of Holy Communion, was visible another completely different aspect of Padre Pio: a dynamic, paternal Padre Pio, whose great eyes roved constantly among all the humanity he saw about him, gazing at one, studying another intently, all these spiritual children so in need of his help, of his direction, of his illumination.

This hour had a particular charm and fascination for all who stood grouped about that confessional and enclosed in that little church. People of all ages and types, from all parts of the world, and all walks of life. Each one wrapped in his own particular mystery and mysterious reason as to why he, rather than another, had found his way to this desolate, unknown spot to be included in the sphere of those great, black, knowing eyes, and, under the tenderly penetrating gaze of Our Lady of Divine Grace who, from above the altar, sweetly bent her head and cast a fleeting, elusive smile over all.

This, her sanctuary, where for four hundred years she had contented herself to stay quietly above that altar. How many secrets she must have whispered in Padre Pio's ears! Secrets that only the Mother of God can know; the Mother of humanity, whose mission is that of introducing, with the softest of feminine guile, that Divine Babe into our hearts. So small, so small—yes but, knowing that once in, if we let Him, He would grow and grow and, with Him, also our hearts. For, as Dr. Sanguinetti was to explain to me one evening as I met him, perhaps for the first time, along the road in the semi-darkness: she was the road our Divine Lord chose to come to us and she still is the road that leads to Him. Something of Him will always be hidden until we have found her.

*Our Surroundings.*

When the long morning activities drew to an end and the noon hour approached, we were on our way to a very much needed lunch. The restaurants down the road toward which we hurried with hope in our hearts each day, numbered a grand total of two. One was run by Mario, the Egyptian, an enormously fat individual with a great head of hair worn pompadour fashion, and his very pretty Hungarian wife, an ex-dancer whom he had met in Egypt. I shall never know how or why they ever ended up at, or discovered, San Giovanni Rotondo, for even though we became very friendly throughout the years, strangely enough this subject was never touched upon. But there they were and there they remained with their luck varying, up and down. (Mario passed away only recently but I believe his widow and two boys are still there.) They were later to change quarters several times but at the period of our first visit they had rented a room on a ground floor that opened up on a small porch-like entrance. From this, with the help of a few wooden boards, emerged the " Restaurant."

The restaurants floor consisted of the good earth under our feet and the walls of the wooden boards already mentioned. It was certainly not windproof, nor coldproof. On high were two windows, small square pieces of glass with two pieces of wood fashioned in cross formation to hold the glass in place. Incorporated in the restaurant was an old well with chain and bucket which formed the constant center of movement and activity—one person coming to draw drinking water, another to fill the nearby basin to rinse off his hands, after which the residue would simply be emptied upon the handy, absorbent floor.

As we would sit huddled, with our feet lifted from the ground on the rung of our wooden chairs, I could not help remembering certain old time movies of my childhood, depicting the " gold rush " days in Alaska. I had seen cabin scenes such as this in them (without the well, of course!). We almost always ate there at noon. The food was fair, better than the atmosphere and limited kitchen facilities would indicate. From the ceiling hung a single electric light bulb on a wire, but the true warmth and cheer came from Mario who moved his huge, bulky form (close to three hundred pounds, I should guess) from table to table to take everyone's order, help serve, and converse. Mario had a gentleman's charm. He seemed to rise with complete nonchalance above any and all surroundings of the various restaurants which he opened and closed in the years to follow. The same can be said of his pretty wife with her interesting foreign accent. Whenever they opened a new restaurant we would always hurry to patronize it. Even when they were down on their luck and she would emerge, tired from frying fish and washing dishes in the little more than three foot kitchen, there would always be something about her of a flower-like beauty. She was a woman who could cook but whose profession was not that of a cook. There was something exotic about both of them. I remember once, in one of their " down days," her telling me of going to confession to Padre Pio and confiding to him, besides her discouragement and fatigue, her worries about her four year old son, not having time to take care of him, or watch over him sufficiently with all the other chores she had to attend to, and Padre Pio saying to her, consolingly, not to worry, that he would watch over the child for her—would protect him.

Not many days afterwards she heard terrified screams emerge from the road above, and people scurrying as they do when there is an accident. She arrived on the scene in time to see, to her horror, her child being pulled out from under the huge truck that had passed over him, dusty, but fortunately none the worse for his experience. When, a few days later, she went again to Padre Pio and reprovingly reminded him of the promise he had made regarding the boy, Padre Pio calmly answered, " And did anything happen to him? Was he hurt? " " No," she answered. " Well," commented Padre Pio dryly, " and so! "

At night, instead of going to Mario's we hurried down the road to the other restaurant which had four normal walls and was windproof, with a very slight bit of heat, but which could very aptly have borne the title of " School of Patience." I must admit this was the scene of numerous impatient tantrums, especially on my part. The waiter was a young boy of perhaps fourteen, stoical and expressionless. Every night more or less the same scene repeated itself. If, for example, one ordered a glass of beer and a portion of roast with potatoes, begging him to bring these three things together, not more than two minutes would pass before he arrived with the beer—where-upon you would explain again, but to no avail. After another pause he would arrive with a dish of greasy potatoes, but no meat. If you were fortunate, after seven or eight minutes the roast (of a sort) finally made its appearance. You could say what you wished, insult him in any way, but he continued not only to look at you with the same sphinx-like gaze, but would repeat the same procedure night after night. Arriving chilled and tired in the dark autumn evening, with the dreaded hour of my cornhusk mattress in view, I would really become quite exasperated and very often would lose my temper completely. He seemed so totally indifferent and lacking in good will. But later, under the brilliant stars, walking slowly uphill to our pensione, I would always repent a little for my behavior, thinking perhaps he was truly a bit stupid and not malicious as it would seem, and wondering from what sort of a family background he came. (This restaurant scene is mentioned only because it is connected with my confession to Padre Pio.)

In the afternoons, on one or two occasions, we walked the two miles to the local village of San Giovanni Rotondo to buy a few needed articles, but more specifically to visit the tombs of Padre Pio's parents, as it was the custom of most pilgrims to do. The tombs had been donated by his spiritual sons and daughters and were inscribed with beautiful and inspiring words. Then there was the quaint cemetery to visit, where on all sides there was evidence of the whitewash paint that each spring the village people were wont to spread everywhere, homes included, in order to freshen and renovate their modest surroundings. In some cases the whitewash was applied with care and precision, and in others splashed with great abandon, but always it contrasted sharply with the somber dark green of the cypress trees which flanked the gravel paths. Everywhere appeared a strange local type of baby angel, fashioned of wrought iron (of nineteenth century, Victorian inspiration—very " ingénue ".) But mixed with the flashes of white described above they helped pour a sweet, simple serenity over the atmosphere of tombs, chapels and graves which otherwise might have been very heavy and lugubrious, containing as they did, so many photographs of the deceased, and reflecting the attitude toward death of a populace that still carried on with the idea of draping themselves and all possible things in black.

But the truly great excursion of our entire visit to San Giovanni Rotondo was to Monte Sant'Angelo, to the very ancient, (fifth century, to be exact) grotto sanctuary of the Archangel St. Michael, about thirty-five miles distant. But of this we will speak at more length in a chapter dedicated to St. Michael and the grotto which will include a bit of the historical background. Certain it is that it was impossible not to observe how strangely this poor, primitive little city seemed to have been preserved—almost cut off—from a fast moving world, awaiting discovery anew, like a spiritual oasis in a time of upheaval, of great need. Need such as our poor, whirling world experiences, at present, so proud of its great scientific progress, of its great intelligence, and yet so incapable of resolving its brotherly problems.

## MARY PYLE

It was on our first trip to San Giovanni Rotondo that we had our first encounter with Mary Pyle and with Dr. Sanguinetti and his charming wife, Signora Emilia, figures known all around the world and mentioned inevitably in every book written about Padre Pio. For this reason we will speak of them only briefly, assuming that the majority of persons already know of them.

Suffice it to say for the present and for those who have by chance never heard of Mary, that she is American, from a wealthy Protestant and socially prominent family. Already converted to Catholicism, she came to San Giovanni Rotondo a good many years ago with Maria Montessori, whose assistant she had become. She was immediately greatly impressed by Padre Pio (who had but shortly before received his stigmata,) by his words and other happenings. She came again and then, as she very humorously told me, " While bathing one fine summer day in the waters of Capri, I suddenly said to myself, " Mary, what are you doing here floating foolishly up and down with the waves when up there at San Giovanni Rotondo is a real live saint, so in need of cooperation and assistance? " That was that. She decided, and up she came to a San Giovanni Rotondo that was indeed, at that time, a rustic, out of the world place lacking everything—roads, light and water. Up she came, heroically, armed with six languages, a musical education and a great love of music, years of study in the best of American private schools, a knowledge of the Montessori system of education, well-travelled, accustomed from childhood to every luxury. She became a member of the Third Order of St. Francis and having established herself among such poor people, decided she could truly serve them only if she were dressed at least as poorly as they. So, removing her lovely dress, she donned a plain brown Franciscan habit, such as the monks wear, put a similar white cord around her waist and there she was, ready for action—all her clothing problems solved.

She built a simple villa and became one of Padre Pio's main secretaries, corresponding with people from every part of the globe in many languages. She played hostess to countless pilgrims who, in order to reach Padre Pio, found themselves almost lost in the semi-wilderness of this out-of-the-world locality.

On the ground floor of her house was a large room which served all purposes. There was a long refectory table, and anyone who wandered in was always welcome to share the simple meal. At this table she also sat to write letters for the poor illiterate women of San Giovanni Rotondo who came up to ask her help. At this table she played " Lotto " and other games for prizes with the youngsters who came up on foot from the town two miles below, to be catechized as well as entertained. Also, and most frequently of all, girls to practice singing and learn hymns, grouped about the small hand organ that formed part of the furnishing of the modest room. Mary, with immense patience, gradually developed them into the choir that sang for many years so delightfully in the little church. She transposed the music and adjusted all things with that perfect taste and sureness that only a person of her background and training could do, inflamed by the love of God. Immense, her work in every field.

Among the persons to whom she extended hospitality were Padre Pio's parents. It was in her villa that each one suffered his last illness, and under her roof and vigilant, merciful eye, that both drew their last breaths. Padre Pio would come to visit them mounted on a mule—the narrow, rocky, dusty path leading from the convent to her house being too rugged and steep for his bleeding feet. She built a Capuchin seminary and convent church at Pietrelcina, Padre Pio's birthplace. But, above all, I think her really great work was the moral help, encouragement, and enlightenment she brought into the lives of so many persons in moments of great darkness, misery, and anguish of all kinds, putting them in contact with Padre Pio even though many times only by correspondence, sending them his words of counsel, prayer and blessing. How many pleasant hours I was to pass in months and years to come with Daisy and my mother in Mary's franciscan house, or in her little garden, listening to her witty and humorous conversation. Sometimes we spoke of the New York social life, her Harvard University brothers, the stag line at the various dances and debuts, etc. But, most of all, we spoke of Padre Pio. She would tell us anecdote after anecdote. Upon her death, there will probably emerge many of the most interesting of all stories concerning him. I think, I do hope, she has kept a record of at least some of these stories. On one occasion she told us of a letter that had traveled from San Giovanni Rotondo to Turin (perhaps twelve or fourteen hundred miles distant) in half an hour. A man from Turin came to San Giovanni Rotondo for a counsel (I don't know of what nature,) but the answer had to be received in Turin before a certain day and hour or it would be useless. Although he stopped a number of days, his road was always blocked and, for some reason, he was never able to reach Padre Pio to obtain his precious answer until almost the hour it should have arrived in Turin. Upon receiving Padre Pio's answer, he sadly remarked that it arrived too late, there not being even the time or possibility of a telegram or phone call from rustic San Giovanni Rotondo. " Well," said Padre Pio, " Write the letter and mail it anyway." " But, Padre-." " I said, write the letter and mail it immediately! " The man obeyed and in half an hour it was received in Turin in time for it to be useful, to serve its purpose. On the envelope, said Mary, clearly visible, was the post-mark of San Giovanni Rotondo with the hour of departure, the post-mark of Turin, and the hour of arrival—an interval of one-half hour. This letter, especially the envelope, is being carefully preserved.

I am going to conclude these few words concerning Mary Pyle before my pen runs away from me and I begin writing the pages that are still inside of me. Let us simply meditate a little on her prayer and penance filled life, on her simplicity, her perseverance, and on the thousands of people whom she helped in every type of tribulation. It would seem that Mary had one day thoroughly read a book called the Gospels.


## CONFESSION MORNING


Finally dawned the morning of our confession with Padre Pio. It is impossible to describe the moment, especially for me who had had so many mystical experiences, encounters and meetings with him before this physical one. All I can remember of my pre-confession emotion was that I knew, had been advised, to wait for the termination of the confession before asking for counsel regarding the solution of the torturing problem for which I had come. Also, because of all these past graces and experiences, I felt completely understood and prepared to accept without a moment of doubt or hesitation, whatever road he indicated for me to follow, or advice he saw fit to give me.

Regarding the normal part of the confession, I felt rather blank and awed, and don't know exactly how I would have fared had he not understood my state of mind and shown me very clearly that he did understand by taking the situation completely in hand, and, by so doing, confirming again all these pre-confession experiences and knowledge of my needs. Outside of saying little more than a " yes " or " no," I did not utter a word. In less than two minutes I had confessed, been counseled and was out of the confessional.

His opening words took care of everything. " Parlo io," (" I will do the talking ",) after which he began reciting my sins to me, pausing between each one so that I could confirm it by saying " Si, padre," (" Yes".) Among these, when he said, " You have been impatient and lost your temper," adding, " ma te ne sei subito pentita " (" but you immediately repented ",) I suddenly had a vision of that little waiter and the greasy potatoes. " Lo spero," (" I hope I did ") I replied, whereupon in a dominating, commanding voice he said, " Ho detto che ti sei subito pentita " (" I SAID that you repented right away ".) In other words, he was not asking—he was telling me. And then suddenly in the middle of the confession, contrary to custom, and before I had, therefore, the occasion to formulate my question, he gave me the advice I, in that moment, particularly needed. Justly so, I now perceive, because what tormented me most in my problem was really a question of conscience, of " spiritual " values that kept me confused and that I could not by myself resolve—a true calvary (as he said,) a hurdle that only a supernatural hand could have helped me to surmount, just as the dream had announced with its great promise of light from above. " E su questo tuo Calvario," he said, " anche se non ci puoi portare l'allegria — cerca almeno di portarci un po piú di rassegnazione . . . . " (" Even though you cannot bring joy on this, your particular calvary, try at least to bring to it a little more spirit of resignation.")

Upon which he terminated confessing me and the doorlet of the confessional closed, and out I went before I had time to realize what had happened, but feeling lighter, so much lighter than when I went in. For, from his words, I understood that I was spiritually at peace with God.

This took the greatest weight from my mind, and although I still wanted to resolve the situation, it presented itself in another light. I knew I was in good hands, was perfectly understood and that, with time, all the rest would follow.

I was at peace with God. I was at peace with God. This was the basis, the foundation, the only foundation upon which the rest could with time be deciphered. With great emphasis he spoke of the word " Patience."

*Padre Pio seen in confessional, and in the choir loft of the old church.*

Photo Elia

Photo Michele

I understand that to the reader of these pages, ignoring so many things, these words of Padre Pio's may not seem very illuminating, but on this point I will have to ask a little margin of faith because of the missing pieces of my story.


# RETURN TO ROME


And so, after our long train trip, we finally arrived in Rome in the late afternoon looking very much like two poor immigrants from heaven-knows-where. We were, very simply, tired and dirty. During the whole journey, when our conversation was not of Padre Pio and the wondrous new world we had found, this port of comprehension, protection and counsel, we could think and speak of nothing else but the much needed bath that awaited us. As our taxi raced through the densely populated streets of Rome in the late afternoon sunshine toward Daisy's apartment, we felt a bit as two inhabitants of another planet who had suddenly dropped onto this world.

My darling, vivacious mother, and Lina, Daisy's rustic but dignified maid, were waiting for us and, having survived the shock of our state of appearance, both began to smile and to participate happily in the enthusiastic accounts of our experiences. Mother asking question after question while Lina ran from room to room, suitcase to suitcase, amid confusion of clothing, doing all she could to make us comfortable. Finally everything quieted down and each one of us retired to her room and respective bath. All that wonderful soap and hot water!

And later, languidly, that nice warm supper, that immaculately clean table. Lina's home-made noodle soup. Mother's radiant joy at having us with her once again. More reminiscences of the morning's confession, a rosary said intimately together for Padre Pio's intentions and, finally, the wonder of wonders—that strangely marvelous thing called a BED. All the tiredness stacked up for so long making itself suddenly, impertinently felt, coming to the surface against all odds—the soft mattress, linen sheets, down pillows, no alarm to ring at four in the morning. What luxury! Just to be able to lie there without moving until Lina made her appearance at eight-thirty with that breakfast tray. Hot coffee, family silver ... As I slid into deep slumber I was obsessed with the idea of that tray and that breakfast among all those pillows. I could think of nothing else. At that moment there was nothing in my very human horizon but just that. I slept and slept.

However, about five in the morning I began to awaken. Something in my subconscious mind would not let me rest. I must fast from midnight if I would receive Holy Communion. The little church at San Giovanni Rotondo—it was the hour that Padre Pio arrived at the altar of St. Francis, always faithful to his appointment, walking slowly and painfully on those poor stigmatized feet, his stigmatized hands joined in prayer, his great eyes fixed on that crucifix. Arrived to plead our cause, to pray for us. The memory of all the graces and blessings I had received . . . .

But in that dark room, in the silence that still enveloped a sleeping Rome, coupled with my still great fatigue, I felt absolutely glued to that bed. Then something happened. A whole regiment of angels must have arrived. Something helped me lift the weight of those blankets and put my feet on the floor. I lit my little lamp and, in a dazed half stupor, began putting on some clothing, finally my coat, my babushka, then quietly, quietly tiptoe through the living room, the entrance hall, taking the keys hanging near the door, noiselessly removing all the night locks and chains, down the staircase, the " portone," the morning air, the last stars fighting it out with the first signs of a conquering dawn, but a few steps and Via Nomentana, still half-sleeping I walked—walked past Villa Torlonia (Mussolini's villa,) the great Roman umbrella pine trees, the gate locked, the grass growing high, abandoned, past history, past . . . finally the parish church, San Giuseppe, new and simple as an American church, the six o'clock Mass, the Mass of the few, the humble, the poor, the little old ladies, the shawl-covered heads.

Sleepily filled with a great sense of peace to be there, silent prayers, Holy Communion, the mystic union. A crucial moment had been passed. I thanked Our Divine Lord for the grace He had sent me which had moved my feet and steps and brought me there to Him in spite of my weak human nature that was so in need of Him.

Outside again, the grayish morning light, an awakening Rome, the first taxis flying by, people beginning to move about, the work-a-day world with all its problems. How could people endure it without HIS HELP?

Back home . . . up the steps . . . the door quietly opened . . . the keys back on their little hook, all the chains and locks again as they were, stealing through the house still filled with the same hushed sleeping atmosphere, into my room, into my night clothes, into that wonderful bed, and, in two minutes sound asleep, serenely and tranquilly, the five o'clock torment disappeared, and at eight-thirty a happy Lina with her tray opening the shutters—ROMAN SUNSHINE!

And later the three of us . . . , St. Peter's . . . , with its round colonade, two great human arms that embraced us and all others who came; inside of them the mystical arms of the mystical body (Corpo Mistico) that is the Catholic Church, universal, universal! How happy we were that morning—and other mornings during my stay in Rome. Almost mechanically at the termination of other visits to San Giovanni Rotondo, our feet always led us to St. Peter's for our Mass and Holy Communion, it seeming the harmonious note upon which to conclude our visit to that mystical world.

I had always loved St. Peter's, and the square, but now, after San Giovanni Rotondo, I suddenly saw it with new eyes. I felt it in a newly-awakened way just as I began seeing everything from a new point of view.

The humble little nun, silently working in a kitchen, or among the poor or aged, or among children, had had in some way revealed to her also the mystic world that had but so recently unveiled itself to me with such generosity. In her heart, despite her tribulations, inner joy and peace.

That poor blind beggar, sitting on the church steps, if armed with prayer and faith, so much richer than that fabulously wealthy person, envied by the eyes of an unthinking world, should he have become disconnected from the true spiritual values, from prayer, from faith—at the very bottom of his beart, boredom and an empty sadness.

My memory raced back to my Philadelphia college days to that crowded New York bound weekend train, to the dining car, to that table for four assigned to my roommate and me, to the other two occupants—Jeanne Eagles, the famous actress, and her secretary. She, playing in the hit of the year, Somerset Maugham's " Rain." I remember the lipstick-red dress, the name " Jeanne " embroidered at the neck, the huge emerald on her finger, the mink coat, on her shoulders the inevitable orchid, her blond, curly head, Peg and I looking at her with wide, wondering eyes, and I am certain a bit of envy of a sort, thinking she truly had everything one could desire and then, a few weeks later, our shocked astonishment when, in the paper, in great black letters, the latest news—" Jeanne Eagles Suicide! "

Such things happen every day but that particular case left an indelible impression, and formed one of my first profound conclusions: the world is not what it appears to be to our unthinking, superficial, easily confused human eye. So much is always hidden.

And so ended our first trip to San Giovanni Rotondo,

a trip that for the first few years was repeated almost every three months, if not accompanied by Daisy, by other persons from the Riviera.

Always new experiences, new enlightenment, each confession with a word, a counsel that, like a bud, would burst into bloom, unfolding itself with the passing of time.

So much there would be to narrate, impossible to even touch upon or this book would never end.

Part III

# A WIDENING ROAD

## NEW ENCOUNTERS
## ANGELIC WORLD
## OTHER STORIES

# "Credo"

For the many people who might be tempted to think of Padre Pio as merely a mind reader, I would like, before proceeding further, to clarify this mistaken idea by making evident how often he knows and is completely aware of, the unknown sides of a situation to which one is referring; the part, that is, that one personally ignores and therefore does not have in mind for him to read.

While this can be seen over and over again in many of these pages, I have thought it well to make a point of it by citing, and translating to the best of my ability, an account of such an experience by an Italian writer, a young priest by the name of Father Alessandro Lingua, who wrote a booklet entitled " Credo," in which he describes, in diary form, the happenings of four " fortunate " as he says, trips to San Giovanni Rotondo.

The complete title is " Credo nella Potenza Redentrice della Sofferenza e della Preghiera di Padre Pio da Pietrelcina " (i.e., " I Believe in the Redeeming Force of the Sufferings and Prayers of Padre Pio of Pietrelcina ".) This book has the Nihil Obstat and Imprimatur of the Catholic Church so I can quote with mind at ease.

Father Lingua made a thousand mile trip to visit Padre Pio, with a busload of thirty or more persons, on a pilgrimage. Besides his desire to make a good confession and receive the spiritual counsel necessary for himself he, as well as a number of others, had come also to implore the grace, or perhaps I should say, almost miracle, of the cure of a desperately sick person (a priest still, I believe, rather young.) I quote:

> " Hesitantly, before my turn, my colleague, another priest, enters the confessional to ask prayers for the recovery of our sick one. The answer is the one very often given: " Accept the will of God. " He raises his eyes to the skies. It is my turn, and I enter the confessional. I open my heart and tell him all there is therein, and yet he looks deeply into my eyes and, with insistance, makes me reveal that which in the emotion of the moment I had forgotten. Terrible yet salutary acuteness; nothing hidden from him—he who penetrates, reads one's heart.

> Having received absolution, I implore the grace I so strongly desire. " Your friend has already told me " he says.

> " I know it," I reply, unsatisfied, " but after a trip of a thousand miles . . . ! "

> Almost annoyed: " You, too, must abandon yourself to the will of God, do you understand? On the other hand, if he has already made a gift offering of his life to God . . . ! " Abruptly, he ceases to speak and looks profoundly into my eyes. Suddenly I understand: THE PROBLEM HAD ALREADY BEEN SOLVED. He raises his arms,

his lips move, and with almost a gesture of dismissal says, " No, no—not cures but conversions."

Comforted, though partly mystified. I again kissed his hand with intense emotion. As my lips drew near to it I smelled very strongly the odor of the blood that escaped from the wound, and that strange perfume, combined with his piercing eyes, penetrated profoundly, indelibly one might say, into my soul. I departed with his promise of prayers, bearer of consolation and spiritual joy.

As soon as I arrived at Fossano, I rushed to the hospital. I found my friend in a sinking condition. Upon seeing me, he smiled and feebly murmured. " Did you see him? Thank you for your postal." " Tell me," I ask almost abruptly, " have you made a gift offering of your life to God? "

Such an audacious question necessitated too intimate an answer. He looked at me with his great eyes still vivid, and simulating a smile said, " What are you talking about? No, No . . . ." He was trying to find a way to avoid my question and then I, abruptly impatient as I am, said, " Listen, my friend, I do not want to force you but, at this moment either you on your deathbed are lying or Padre Pio is lying."

My words produced a strong reaction and bursting forth with as much force as his condition would permit, and as one who wanted to be liberated from a tormenting secret said: " Yes, yes. Two years ago I offered my life to God for a seminary student and for my ' Cenacoline ' (a religious order of nuns founded by him.) I am happy to know that Padre Pio confirms that God has accepted my offer. Thank you. You will be in the first row of those remembered . . . ."

Deeply moved, I reverently withdrew from his bedside. I was fatigued, but my thoughts flew away to him—to Padre Pio, man become spirit—a true apostle of light and truth."

# Miracle of a rosary

The first person from Chiavari (the town where I live) with whom I went to Padre Pio was Signora Flora Riggio, a concert pianist graduated from the Milan Conservatory of Music and wife of Dottore Orfeo Riggio, director of the local prisons and formerly director of the prisons in Genoa.

Orfeo was, let us say, a " border-line " Catholic, accompanying his wife to the church door each Sunday and returning to walk home with her after Mass. A very fine, upright and charitable man, he had always done his utmost to see that justice was done to all prisoners, improving the meals and the social and moral conditions as much as it was in his power to do. And so, even though he had not yet fully discovered the first commandment—the love of God above all other persons and things—he was well on the way to observing the second commandment so similar to the first—" Love your neighbor as yourself."

Maybe it was for this reason God smiled in his direction and manifested Himself in a special way in order to win him over, knowing his youthful religious education and training had been of a limited nature.

I will pass, for the present, recounting many manifestations of perfumes, etc., which he had received before I departed for San Giovanni Rotondo with his wife Flora. Something about Padre Pio impressed him favorably and he was very willing that his wife should go with me and gladly gave her the money for the trip.

It was the year 1951, soon after the war, and the means of transportation were not as yet abundant, nor even normal as they are now, so after an adventuresome and tiring trip we finally arrived at San Giovanni Rotondo where Flora, with her delicate artistic temperament, felt more than others perhaps, the rarefied spiritual air. This, coupled with the longer than usual wait for our confession, made her nervous and undecided as to whether or not to wait for our turn. (The devil is always very active at San Giovanni Rotondo, bent on trying to keep people from contact with Padre Pio.)

But evidently our friend and protector, St. Michael the Archangel won, for she stayed. On the morning of her confession there was, because of the feast day, music in the little church which pleased her, and when she entered the confessional Padre Pio was waiting paternally for her and said with understanding: " And so, those thoughts and worries have returned after many years to torment you . . . . " *He already knew every-thing.* She emerged with a serenity and peace never before attained—the prize of victory, of having persevered.

One day, while we were conversing with a young lady whom I knew very well, Dr. Sanguinetti's secretary, I happened to be holding in my hand a small gold rosary, the one I had been given on the day of my first Holy Communion. " Give it to me and I will see to it that Padre Pio will receive it and use it to say a round of the rosary." Joyfully I accepted her offer. Only now Flora confides to me that on those nervous, pre-confession days she had become obsessed by the desire to possess a rosary like mine—that is, one on which Padre Pio had prayed. Her mind kept reverting to a beloved rosary she had at home which she had purchased on the feast of the Holy Cross in her parish a number of years before and which, being broken in at least four places, she had reluctantly and sadly discarded, having carefully wrapped it in fine tissue paper and put it in a corner of the top drawer of a small chest.

Upon our return to Chiavari, Flora spoke with enthusiasm of her trip, of Padre Pio, and of the great hospital —" Casa Sollievo della Sofferenza "—which had begun to take shape and which Padre Pio was anxious to complete in order to relieve the suffering of so many people who, living in the radius of miles from there, had no adequate means of good hospitalization. When she offered to return to her husband the 10,000 lire left over from the trip, he refused it, saying, " Send it to Padre Pio for his hospital," and so she brought it to me with these words, " when you send your monthly offering to Padre Pio, include this for us." This I did.

After ten days or so I received a letter of acknowledgement and thanks signed by Dr. Sanguinetti, which also contained these words, " . . . Il padre fa sapere che non si allontana giammai né da lei, né dai suoi cari . . . ." (Padre Pio makes it known that he is constantly near to you and to your dear ones.)

I was happy and waited eagerly to see what he would say in his letter to them, their names and addresses having been carefully listed so that an individual answer could be sent. A week passed, then two, then three, but no answer did they receive. I could not understand what had happened and felt quite annoyed, not so much because of the unacknowledged gift, but chiefly because of the personal words that would have pleased them. I thought about this constantly and one day, passing before Flora's door, the words in my reply letter suddenly returned to me with new significance. I rang the bell, Flora opened the door, and I entered the small reception hall. " Flora," I hurried to say, " Dr. Sanguinetti says in my answer, ' Il padre makes it known that he never leaves you (always is close) to you and your dear ones.' Evidently, instead of writing he will make it known in some way that he is near you." With these words, a wonderful perfume began to encircle us. A perfume of roses! At first I did not give this any importance, thinking that, as on many other occasions, there were flowers in the adjacent sitting room. The perfume persisted, becoming stronger—so strong that it interrupted my thoughts and conversation. " Flora," I asked, " have you some roses in the next room? " " Not a flower in the house," she replied. She too noticed the perfume. We both stood in silence for a moment—

impressed. " This is evidently a confirmation of what I have just said, that is, that Padre Pio will manifest his nearness in some way, and much sooner than we expect! "

I now pass the pen to my friend Flora who will tell the remainder of the story in her own words:

" And so it happened. The day after Clarice assured me that something of an extraordinary nature was about to happen, I found myself in the bathroom in the act of brushing my hair before going to bed when suddenly I became surrounded by perfumes and felt almost pushed by a mysterious force into my bedroom. My husband was already in bed. Scarcely understanding what I was doing, I went to the little chest in the drawer of which I kept the beloved, broken rosary. Opening the drawer, I found the piece of paper in which the rosary had been wrapped was almost completely unfolded. My fingers touched the rosary and, extracting it from its place, I lifted it on high and before my stupefied eyes there it was—whole! It seemed new and I could not help repeating again and again, " It looks like new! It looks like new! " Later Clarice and I examined the rosary together, and much to our marvel, could not deny that it seemed fixed by a more than human hand, so delicately and perfectly had it been repaired. Almost as a signature and in confirmation of the miracle, one " Hail Mary " had been deliberately left out. It was one of the three at the end of the rosary. It was half attached to its proper place next to the other two, but it was decidedly outside the completely closed chain.

Had it been repaired by a human hand, after so much time and delicate work certainly the person in question would have completed the whole operation by inserting the Ave Maria as it presented much less difficulty than the other repairs. Had it been new, certainly the " Hail Mary " would not have been missing.

In confirmation of the truth of this happening and giving our word that not one of the four of us in the house had touched, fixed, substituted, or had repaired this rosary, we, the four members of the household, at this time wish to sign our names.

> Flora Podesta Riggio (myself)
> Orfeo Riggio (my husband)
> Ines Podesta (my sister)
> Giuseppina Passarelli (our maid)

I often smile to myself when many, upon hearing about this experience say, in a superficial manner, " Oh, it was probably her husband who had it repaired." This smile comes to my lips particularly when repeating these words to Orfeo. He, too, smiles to himself: " Certainly, if anyone had told me of such a happening, I, too, would have said the same thing and instead this is absolutely not the case .... "

Later, in November 1953, he was transferred to Ancona as director of the penal institutions there which were much larger than those at Chiavari and numbered,

I believe, several hundred inmates. At his entrance into office very few of the prisoners assisted at religious services on Sunday. As was his habit, in trying to reorganize all conditions for the better, this time he collaborated actively with the chaplain and added the spiritual side to the social side of the prison activities. He distributed Padre Pio's little periodical " Casa Sollievo della Sofferenza " among the prisoners, and prayer-books entitled " Seguendo la Santa Messa " (Following the Holy Mass,) together with photographs of Padre Pio. Gradually, a great number of them began to find their way back to God, and more and more attended Mass on Sunday and received Holy Communion, coming also on the first Fridays of the month. When the bishop came to offer their Easter Mass, more than three-quarters received the Holy Eucharist, fulfilling their Easter duty.

Orfeo accompanied his wife in pilgrimage to San Giovanni Rotondo, went to confession to Padre Pio and to Holy Communion. He has continued throughout the years not only to accompany his wife to the church door but also to enter and to assist at the Holy Sacrifice of the Mass with her. All four are now members of our prayer group.

The little miracle of a mended rosary indeed wrought larger spiritual miracles of conversion.

# A moving grace

The second person with whom I went to San Giovanni Rotondo from Chiavari was Flora's aunt, Cornelia Zolezzi, who at the time lived in the apartment above Flora.

The latter's only daughter Lelia was, at the moment, in South America on a business trip and Cornelia was alone with her maid. I say " alone " and yet " not alone " for, during the war years she had lived in Florence with Lelia and sublet her Chiavari apartment to a very nice woman whom we will call Signora Anna. With the war's end mother and daughter finally decided to re-establish themselves in their Chiavari flat but Signora Anna, a very pleasant and gay woman of mature age, had become very attached to this sunny home, and did not wish to leave. Due to the fact that the quarters were large, with numerous rooms, she was very willing to let the owner share it with her and so each one lived in a part of the house with her own maid, sharing kitchen and bath.

For a while this worked out but soon Cornelia, who had always been accustomed to her own privacy, began to desire ardently to be alone. However, in no way, and with no argument, could she persuade Signora Anna to change her mind and leave. The latter would go about singing gaily and being very affable, but move she would not.

After a year or so the situation became a real cross in Cornelia's life and, with the prospect of her daughter's return, and the guests the two had always entertained, she began to worry constantly about this condition and how to resolve it.

She had a picture of Padre Pio on a table near her bed and one night said she heard a voice call several times, " Cornelia, Cornelia." This decided her. She would go to Padre Pio to implore this favor, that is, that Signora Anna could be persuaded to move. And so we left together for San Giovanni Rotondo.

When we were there, for some reason or other, possibly thinking she had a longer time to wait for confession than she did, she impulsively went to confession to another priest. Two days later, on a Sunday morning, her confession turn arrived. Unless there is a serious reason, Padre Pio refuses to confess the penitent, dismissing him rapidly if there has been less than a week since his last confession.

Cornelia decided to try, however, hoping that once in the confessional she could at least implore the favor she so much desired. But all in vain! Padre Pio did not give her the time or the opportunity, merely saying: " Va, sei in grazia di Dio! " (" Go, you are in the grace of God.",) with which words he closed the small confessional doorlet. She emerged with mixed emotions, happy to hear him say that she was in the state of grace but sad that she had not been able to speak, to implore her favor.

This all happened about eight-thirty in the morning. At the same hour in Chiavari, my aunt, leaning out of her fourth story bedroom window, saw a small moving van across the street before Cornelia's house, and movers running rapidly in and out carrying Signora Anna's furniture. For some reason she had been taken with the idea that she wanted to leave—and immediately! Cornelia was truly, as Padre Pio had said, " In the state of grace," or should we say, " In the state of two graces! "

Coincidence? Perhaps, perhaps not.

# An intellectual succumbs

In the early autumn of the year 1955 or 1956, I was at San Giovanni Rotondo with my mother, my aunt, and my cousin. We met Engineer C. from Milan, who told us his story, his first eventful meeting with Padre Pio a few years before, so humorous and delicately profound in its Franciscan simplicity!

He had had a very serious knee condition for two years which no longer seemed able to improve when, upon finding himself purely by chance, at San Giovanni Rotondo (driving with a journalist friend), he decided, out of curiosity to go to confession to Padre Pio in order to see him and study him at first hand, one might say.

Upon entering the confessional he began: " Padre, I believe in God in my way, but you know . . . . we intellectuals—the idea of going to confession to another man—well, you know—we intellectuals, etc., etc."

He said that Padre Pio continued to look at him silently until finally he had had enough, and raising his gloved hand, let it fall with a good, heavy thud on the top of his head, as one might do in the act of reproving a child. In his soft, annoyed, scolding voice, Padre Pio said: " Suppose you stop all this chatter and begin instead by telling me that it is now twenty years since your last confession and that, since the day when you were married, you have never again received the Blessed Sacrament."

Mr. C. said he remembers counting rapidly in his head—" Yes, yes, my daughter is now nineteen. It is true that it is twenty years . . . . "

Taken so completely by surprise, he finally ended by making a good confession and later as he walked down the road, meditating upon the morning's happenings, he suddenly noticed that he was walking quite well— he was not using his cane, but dangling it on his arm!

Amazed, pleased, and yet wounded in his pride, he rushed up to Dr. Sanguinetti in the growing hospital and, suffused by mixed emotions, protested, " This can't have happened to me! " Dr. Sanguinetti held his sides laughing, " I am sorry but it has really happened to you."

Mr. C. was, at the time of our meeting, one of Padre Pio's most faithful spiritual sons, bringing his wife and two daughters very often with him on his visits to San Giovanni Rotondo. He belongs to, and participates regularly in one of Padre Pio's large prayer groups in Milan—a group which is composed largely of his fellow intellectuals.

# *Vanina*

My friend Vanina is an extremely charming and intelligent woman—married, mother of two grown children, member of a very distinguished and titled family, a university graduate.

I first met her at San Giovanni Rotondo about twelve years ago. She told me that from her girlhood she had been a most devoted spiritual daughter of Padre Pio and with good reason. I will let her recount, in her own words, the intriguing story of her first meeting with Padre Pio.

" When I was preparing for my last examination prior to entering the university, I had some difficulty with mathematics and science, and so I went for private lessons to a well-known professor. This professor was an atheist and while he was an excellent teacher, he very often rambled from the scientific field to the philosophical one. I was sixteen at the time and found all this very disconcerting. I remember that on one occasion he began to ridicule the idea of the Holy Trinity.

It was already towards evening when the lesson ended and finding myself in the vicinity of St. Peter's, I decided to go there to confession.

At that time the tomb of Pope Pius X. was still in the subterranean part of the basilica and, as I was very devoted to him, I decided to go down to say a prayer before confession.

I prayed for the conversion of my professor and also that I might find in the church an excellent confessor, one that would be able to explain, in words my professor would be able to grasp, the mystery of the Holy Trinity.

It was quite late however, and the basilica was on the verge of closing. All the confessionals seemed empty and, upon encountering the custodian, I was told that there were no more confessors available and to return the following day.

Sad and disappointed, I began to wind my way to-wards the entrance, when a Capuchin monk emerged from somewhere and asked me if I wanted to go to confession. Happily surprised, I answered in the affirmative.

He spoke to me wonderfully of the Holy Trinity, explaining all to me with clear and simple words. I was very pleased and satisfied. As I neared the exit, I again met the man charged with closing the church who seemed quite amazed when I told him that I had found a confessor.

Not long afterwards, I found myself, among friends, speaking of a difficult problem that preoccupied me at the time. One of these friends advised me to go to Padre Pio for counsel. When I was shown a photograph of him, I immediately recognized my confessor of that evening in St. Peter's. My friends, however, insisted that I was mistaken, telling me that Padre Pio never left the convent at San Giovanni Rotondo. Therefore I decided that the shadowy hour in St. Peter's had confused me and so put the thought completely out of my mind.

About a year later, I had the opportunity of going, together with a group of fellow students, to San Giovanni Rotondo for the first time. During the day we found ourselves, with other persons, in a room where Padre Pio was to pass in order to give us his blessing. He appeared, and made his way among us. Reaching me, he suddenly stopped and, pointing in my direction, said, " I already know you." Whereupon I replied, " No Padre. I have never come here before." " But," he replied, " don't you remember that evening in St. Peter's? "

## I had first met him in bilocation!

Later, when I went to confession, Padre Pio said to me, " Your father died the day you were born and it is since that day that I have been praying for you." From that moment I have never abandoned Padre Pio, finding in him not only my spiritual guide and counselor but also, in a way, an almost human father, replacing the one I had never known.

A few years later during one of my confessions, I told him that I was sometimes a bit scrupulous, especially regarding the saying of my penance. Either because I became distracted or in fear that I had not said the exact number of prayers prescribed, very often I would begin to recite them all again. This annoyed Padre Pio very much, and he reprimanded me severely, saying that if I did not overcome the scrupulous habit, and if I ever fell into this error again, he would give me a " schiaffone "—a good sound slap.

Some months later, when in Naples, I went to confession in an almost empty church. Upon terminating, I went to the main altar railing to recite my penance. At the end of this exercise, my old scrupulous habit returned and, fearing that I had not said them properly, decided to repeat them. Scarcely had I begun when I was interrupted by a most resounding slap in the face. So resounding was it that, as I stood up, shocked and confused, my confessor looked out of his confessional and, as I hastened to leave the church, said to me. " E che è mai stato? " (And whatever was it that happened?)

' Just a " bello schiaffone,' I replied. Padre Pio had truly demonstrated his paternity! "

Perhaps, the dramatic story of Vanina's birth will be of interest to the reader at this point.

Vanina's mother was a very spiritual and religious person while her father was not only irreligious, but belonged to a strongly anti-clerical organization that was very prevalent at that period. For years her mother prayed and prayed for the conversion of her husband.

During her husband's last illness, she was expecting their sixth child, Vanina. At that time, they were at their country estate.

When her mother was toward the eighth month of pregnancy, one evening her father took a slight turn for the better and seemed tranquil. Her mother, taking advantage of the respite, sent all the tired servants to bed. They had been keeping vigil night and day over their sick " padrone " and were exhausted, so she decided to sit up with him herself that night. At a certain hour, a dog down in the courtyard began howling and wailing in a most disturbing manner. In order to quiet him by letting him come indoors, she, being a very courageous woman, hurried down alone and, in order to save time, passed through the stables. During this passage, she was suddenly overcome with severe pain and, before she could call for help or find her way up to the house, Vanina made her appearance in this world. (Not only was Our Divine Lord born in a stable, but also by chance St. Francis of Assisi.)

As her mother, half fainting, dragged herself up the stairs with her newborn child in her arms, she remembered seeing in a corner of the staircase, standing in the shadows, a Franciscan monk with his hood pulled up over his head. In the emotion of the moment and of the night, however, this passed into her subconscious mind, and it was only after many months that she recalled the monk again.

The alarmed servants sent for the doctor who, after

caring for Vanina's mother, found her father in a sinking state and now desirous of a priest and of making his peace with God.

The priest was called but members of the anti-clerical group to which her father had belonged stood guard at the gate of the villa so as to block his entrance. When he said, however, that he had been called hurriedly to baptize a prematurely born infant, they stood aside to permit him to enter. Once inside, he hurried to the bedside of the dying man in time to administer the last sacraments.

Thus it was Vanina's birth that permitted this important spiritual encounter for her father. And her mother's long years of prayer had been answered. From that day (as was later confirmed by Padre Pio,) God had placed Vanina under the protective eye and prayer of Padre Pio!

Truly a modern version of the " Little Flowers of St. Francis."

# Gemma di Giorgi: 1967

I had so often heard of, and read the story of little Gemma di Giorgi, the child born blind without pupils in her eyes—declared incurable and inoperable by one specialist after another, who at the age of seven (in 1947) was brought to Padre Pio by her discouraged, yet somehow hopeful grandmother, and who returned home from her trip, still without pupils in her eyes as when she left, but with her eyesight mysteriously functioning! She is now about twenty-eight years old and I often wondered what had become of her through all these years. Did she still see? Had pupils gradually formed in her eyes or was she still lacking them as when she was born?

For this reason I was very happy when destiny or chance, or call it what you will, presented her to me on my trip to San Giovanni Rotondo in May of 1967. A gracious, attractive young woman, who despite the fact that her eyesight functions, still has those foggy, strange looking eyes that are a characteristic of the blind.

We spoke together on numerous occasions, and she told me of some of her humorous experiences because of this eye condition. Among these are the eye examinations that she still undergoes occasionally by well known specialists who are all agreed that there is no remedy for her condition: without pupils in one's eyes, one cannot see and therefore blindness will have to continue, etc. When they have finished their diagnosis and discourses and she announces that she can see and that it is a miracle obtained through the prayers and intercession of Padre Pio, their incredulous reactions are often amusing.

When I told her that I was putting together some " testimonials " in honor of Padre Pio and asked her to tell me with precision of her " miracle," she replied that first she would ask Padre Pio in confession because she makes no move without his permission or consent. For this reason I too am very happy and satisfied because the permission was given and I can therefore hope that this story of Gemma Di Giorgi can do some good in this world, forming part of that mysterious design that we very rarely can see but that the Divine Force above us keeps constantly weaving.

By the way, I may add that during this confession, Gemma, due to the sunny and very windy weather, was wearing sun glasses, and that Padre Pio evidently cannot bear to see her with glasses. " Why," he said as he passed his hand over her eyes, " are you wearing glasses? You see very well."

And now I will return to the original story of how this miraculous happening took place.

It has been written in innumerable books how in 1947, when Gemma was seven years old, after the visit of three eye specialists—Drs. Bonifacio, Cucco and Contini and others who all said the same thing—that she was inoperable; that nothing could be done for her blindness; that she had no pupils in her eyes—her grandmother decided to bring her to Padre Pio to implore a miracle from Our Lady of Divine Grace.

The story dealing with this miracle has been written many times, and, as told to the present is true, but there is one fact that most writers ignore and that had I not had it in writing from Gemma, would never have known myself. But, since Divine Providence saw fit to grant this enormous grace to Gemma in this particular way, I think it best that the complete truth should be revealed because even though we cannot immediately see why it happened in this particular manner, yet there must be a reason, and a very good one, for while we make many mistakes, that great incomprehensible force above us makes all moves only with the most perfect precision!

It is true, as has been written in the accounts of this happening that Gemma's grandmother brought her to Padre Pio. It is true that Padre Pio, although never having had the child presented to him, called Gemma by name before all the congregation at church, heard her confession, and while in the confessional, despite the fact that she made no mention of her blindness, passed his stigmatized hand over her eyes, making the sign of the cross over each eye. It is true that he gave her, that same day, her first Holy Communion. It is true that, at the end of the confession, as he blessed her, he said: " Sii buona e santa." (" Be good and saintly.") All this, as has already been written, is true.

The fact that has been omitted in the articles I have read so far, is that Gemma's eyesight began mysteriously functioning on the train trip that was bringing her from Sicily to San Giovanni Rotondo to visit Padre Pio.

About half way there, Gemma began seeing the sea and a steamship, and remarked of this to her grandmother— whereupon the grandmother and other pilgrim friends who were accompanying them, all marveled, and began speaking of a miracle, and praying. However, the after-the-war trip from Sicily to Foggia was very long, difficult and tiresome and, while Gemma's grandmother observed the " miracle " that had taken place, she saw these things through a pair of extremely tired and exhausted eyes. So much so that, when she arrived at San Giovanni Rotondo and finally was able to be confessed by Padre Pio, she was in a confused state of mind and still obsessed by the idea of the grace she had come to ask and, as soon as the confession was ended, made haste to implore it of Padre Pio—Gemma's eyesight! In the grandmother's own words:

> " I asked the grace for Gemma and I told him that the child was weeping because, in her confession with him, she had forgotten to ask this grace " I will never forget his soft and tender voice as he answered me with these words: ' Do you have faith, my daughter? The child must not weep and neither must you for the child sees, and you know she sees.' I understood then that Padre Pio was alluding to the sea and ship Gemma had seen during the trip and that God had used our saintly Padre Pio to break through the darkness that covered Gemma's eyes.

> After Padre Pio had given Gemma her first Holy Communion before all the populace that filled the church, with the same fingers that had held the

Holy Eucharist he again made, for the second time, the sign of the cross over each of Gemma's eyes. And so, finally we started our return trip home but, since the whole trip had been, for me, extremely wearing and exhausting, I was taken by a very high fever and sent to the municipal hospital of Cosenza. As soon as I recovered, I had Gemma's eyes examined by an eye specialist who immediately declared Gemma blind and without pupils. I, poor ignorant person that I am, imagined that now that Gemma could see she should also have pupils in her eyes. I did not understand that even without pupils the child could, through the will of God, be enabled to see just the same. I therefore became confused and worried when I heard the oculist declare Gemma blind. But Gemma even though without pupils, had her eyesight—could see— and so I insisted to the doctor that the child could see. In order to persuade me, the doctor showed Gemma some objects and when she recognized them and showed distinctly and without difficulty that she saw these things, the doctor stamped his foot on the floor and said, 'Without pupils, one cannot see. The child sees; therefore it is a miracle.' Since that time many eye doctors from all over Italy have gotten in contact with me requesting to examine Gemma's eyes. Many have even arrived here in our home and all have declared the same thing: that without pupils in one's eyes one should not be able to see and that, therefore, this is a miracle."

Thus the words of Gemma's grandmother.

So what must we conclude? Simply that while they were traveling to Padre Pio to ask this grace, the grace came to them through the intercession of Padre Pio's prayers and before any human contact had taken place. God, for His own mysterious reasons had wanted it to happen this way.

Supernatural happenings are by their very nature elusive but they do always leave a good margin for pondering and reasoning.

# Dr. Sanguinetti and The Home for the Relief of Suffering

Perhaps to the American mind, accustomed as it is to large well-equipped hospitals, this hospital of Padre Pio's does not signify much, nor does it make a great impression. For this reason it would seem that a few words of explanation are in order.

To begin with, one of the first things to consider is the dearth of good hospitals in southern Italy—still the poorest part of the country. While the government is doing all it can to ameliorate, industrialize and develop this section, building new roads, schools, etc., the program is vast and costly. Despite the enormous progress made during the last twenty years, much still remains to be done with new exigencies arising constantly.

More than twenty years ago, when the first stones were laid for the foundation of the " Casa Sollievo della Sofferenza," conditions were much more deplorable, with the government's whole interest concentrated in a rebuilding program to replace and repair edifices ravaged by the war.

San Giovanni Rotondo, a town of approximately 18,000 inhabitants, contained no hospital and the nearest one, extremely modest and meager, was perhaps thirty miles distant. Even the one of the city of Foggia forty miles away, was antiquated and over crowded.

A good, large modern hospital was a crying necessity and Padre Pio with his enormous heart, suffered with the suffering—deeply preoccupied. Through the intercession of his prayers, sufferings and penance-filled life, graces poured down upon the persons and homes, with the result that offerings in gratitude arrived spontaneously. This was a way of saying " Thank You." Padre Pio, being a Franciscan vowed to poverty could, naturally, not keep even one cent of these offerings. For a number of years these offerings went into various channels of charity but, in 1940, permission was finally granted to use this money to begin the great work he so ardently desired— the building of the much needed hospital. The war intervened however, and it was not until 1946 with the restoration of peace, that it was possible to initiate construction. The original building containing 350 beds was completed on May 5, 1956.

Two new additions have since been made, bringing the total to 800 beds. Incorporated in the building are a chapel and a church, and over a million patients have already received treatment within its walls.

If we remember the words of Our Lord in the Gospel that we can judge a tree by the fruit it bears, that a bad tree cannot bear good fruit, surely this hospital is a tribute to Padre Pio, whose silent sacrifices and union with God have borne such a rich fruit.

Many other types of charitable projects could be the subject of polemical discussion, but certainly not a beautiful hospital—a home where the sick can find care, fraternal love and understanding, united with all the best that science has to offer in the way of the latest and most modern equipment and assistance.

Also, the reader must know that in Italy there is a form of socialized medicine. Working people receive free hospitalization and medical care. However, the sum given the hospital for each patient is very modest with the result that the sick person is usually placed in a large ward with many beds.

Not so in Padre Pio's " Home," where there are two, three and, at most, six beds in a ward. The beautiful and efficient hospital beds are well spaced in the airy, cheerful rooms. Oxygen outlets and radio earphones are placed above each bed. Rich and poor receive the same treatment, food and consideration, even though what each one pays varies considerably and some do not pay at all.

There are five magnificently equipped operating rooms and all the latest and best in x-ray, pathology, therapy, blood bank, etc. Everything is in color; there is no " hospital white." The surroundings are more than pleasing to the eye, with colored marble and tile fusing in many varied shades and nuances. Once, during the building process, good, kindly Carlo Kisvarday (a Yugo-slavian pharmacist who settled at San Giovanni Rotondo to assist Padre Pio in his work) who kept the books, remarked to Padre Pio that, " We are spending too much money on luxuries," received the answer, "Nothing is too good or beautiful for the sick and suffering."

But, after all, perhaps these descriptions of the " Home for the Relief of Suffering " can have true significance not only for those who are aware of what this hospital has cost Padre Pio in heroic personal sacrifice, but also and more emphatically, for the smaller number of us who, from a barren, rocky hillside in a forsaken spot with very limited water and electricity, and against all odds of every type, have seen this great luminous building spring into being through the stubborn heroic dedication of a small group of Padre Pio's spiritual sons, determined to bring to fruition this enormous enterprise. The most important of these is certainly Dr. Sanguinetti (familiarly known as Willy,) whose great mind, capable of handling the many and varied enterprises included in this project, was put completely and humbly at Padre Pio's disposal.

There is an inscription over the door of one of the monks' cells at San Giovanni Rotondo, which reads: " PRAY FOR THE SOULS IN PURGATORY; THEY DID NOT HAVE THE WISDOM TO MAKE GOOD USE OF THEIR TALENT." This is certainly not applicable to Dr. Sanguinetti, whose every talent, and they were many, was consecrated to the highest Christian ideals, consuming himself in this enormous technical work aided by his medical and scientific knowledge, always dynamically patient, persistent and selfless.

No water, no electricity: rocks and dynamite: criticism and complications! Nothing stopped him or was too difficult. Forward he plunged, surmounting all obstacles and, most important of all, everything was done with a great sense of beauty and good taste—not the least of his many talents.

An illustration of these qualities of his can be seen in the hundreds of cypress and pine trees now flourishing on the stony hillside about and above the hospital. Originally, the only green came from low, wild shrubbery, the

*Doctor Guglielmo Sanguinetti*    Photo Abresch

*View of Padre Pio's hospital from belfry of old church.*

Photo Abresch

re-forestation department refusing to act, saying the rocky terrain was unadaptable to trees. With such a verdict others would have abandoned the idea, but not Sanguinetti.

Patiently and persistently he planted one little tree after another, each planting requiring blasts of dynamite to produce a hole large enough to contain the carload of dirt which had to be mule-drawn up the inclining, irregular, roadless ground. And this procedure repeated hundreds of times, and constituting only one of the dozens of problems of every nature and type that he had to meet and resolve. Among these others could be cited the organization and printing of Padre Pio's little bi-monthly newspaper called " Casa Sollievo della Sofferenza." Also, as more and more people, having met him and his charming wife Emilia, would in turn write to them when in need of counsel, knowing that they were in direct contact with Padre Pio, an enormous amount of secretarial work fell upon their broad and willing shoulders. Truly, they were " franciscans! " The door of their simple, little prefabricated home was always open to welcome all who came to unburden themselves, to entreat them to ask Padre Pio this or that, and to relax in the warm, serene environment. For, while the little house was most unpretentious, yet the mere placement of an armchair, a vase of flowers, a picture, revealed the hand of well-bred, highly cultivated persons, producing an overall impression of charm and hospitality that did not have to apologize for itself to even the wealthiest and most aristocratic. Everyone was content there; hosts and house fused in a vibrating cordiality.

My first encounter with Dr. Sanguinetti was on my original trip, one autumn evening as he emerged from the convent door. The road and all surroundings were still poetically in complete darkness, the only light, significantly, over the small, green door of the little church.

In this illumination we were able to see one another. I did not know who he was but I did surmise for, in his arms he carried a large bundle—an enormous red peasant handkerchief, the four corners tied in knots. The inside of the handkerchief was stuffed with paper money, the fruit of Padre Pio's weekly suffering—money for the hospital. I remember that he paused to say a few deeply felt words concerning the Blessed Virgin Mary and of this, her sanctuary.

Perhaps Dr. Sanguinetti can best be described in the words of Carlo Trabucco: *

> " The man I am writing of today is Guglielmo Sanguinetti. He was a doctor, a native of Parma. When death took him, he was about sixty and was living in the ' spur ' of the ' boot ' that is the Italian peninsula. My friend, Guglielmo Sanguinetti, now rests at San Giovanni Rotondo, in the Gargano hills and, if you want information in his regard, refer your queries to Padre Pio.
>
> A man without whom, Padre Pio will tell you, Casa Sollievo della Sofferenza (Home for the Relief of Suffering) would not have sprung into being— a man whom he called friend and considered a

* Translated from article in " Orrizonti " magazine.

brother—words that, from the lips of Padre Pio, have a value (how shall we say?) other than 'complete integrity.' He does not make a gift of these words with facility and, in the number of his true friends, Guglielmo Sanguinetti occupies a place in the front row. I say 'occupies' even though it is more than ten years since he passed away, because Padre Pio does not forget those whom Divine Providence has placed by his side. The first of these, in order of merit, is Sanguinetti, son of the Italian anti-clerical epoch, being born at the end of the 19th century.

At the beginning of the 20th century science was considered above all things. Now that science has traveled another fifty years, and has made remarkable advances, scientists encircle this progress with cautious reserve. But, at the beginning of the century we find Spencer and Conte lording it over the field of international philosophy, and Ardigo in the Italian national world of thought. A student in medical school, Guglielmo Sanguinetti underwrites the principle that 'all is sensation and union of sensations and nothing more.'

How did it come to pass that a young doctor whose practice was in Mugello (outside Florence) found his road to Damascus? By chance, we say. But it is better explained by saying a turn that Providence prepared with foresight in the shape of the expressed desire of his wife, the charming Signora Emilia, to go to see a certain monk who, at that time one heard had received the stigmata as had

St. Francis of Assisi. If his wife was moved in her desire by a religious sentiment, he, indifferent to spiritual problems, was moved by a medical curiosity to look into the facts of the case. As soon as they reached San Giovanni Rotondo, he attempted to penetrate into the convent but was thrown out, rather rudely, by a lay brother. I will now take a few lines from my diary:

' He went to bed and the next morning took his place early in church in order to see Padre Pio nearby. When he saw him, he said a word of salutation which was exchanged brusquely by a word of invitation: " Wait." He waited until the next day; he went to confession and he came to the conclusion that the monk had not been an " inquisitor " but rather a brother. With that confession was buried, all at once, the man of the past and —significantly—there was suddenly born a man who passed from the role of an unknown to that of a friend—a friend whom this fisherman of souls had brought to shore in order to make of him a fellow traveller. " This is your road. Walk! " He could not know, nor could he penetrate, the meaning of Padre Pio's words as he gazed deeply into his eyes which were at the same time gentle and imperious. " You must come here. We will put up three tents: one for Jesus, one for you and one for me." He is literally flabbergasted. His mind works but no conclusion emerges. " You will remain here always! " He understands always less. It is certain that, after that confession extraordinary things take place inside of him. He does some mental calculating: not since the year 1910 had he gone to confession, and that was twenty-five years ago. He is now forty-one years old. He had been in the army for four years during the war; had fought with the Infantry of the Pinerolo brigade; had won a pair of war decorations. He had known— and had had to deal with people of every rank and file, had fought and won; had found himself in serious, even tragic situations and had never trembled. Yet now before this strange man, he trembles. Fright? Nonsense! He trembles because he is aware that inside of himself there is a crumbling, crashing ruin. Forty years of life are falling to pieces and, in those ruins are the ideas that had governed his life. Now he not only rejects them, but is unable to understand how he had ever accepted them. An authentic "Waterloo!" '

From that day everything changed. But the war came again, and the ' tent ' was not pitched. In 1946, with the return of peace, Dr. Sanguinetti returned from Mugello to San Giovanni Rotondo with the intention of staying eight days. He remained eight years until death came unexspectedly to claim him.

Those eight years gave birth to ' Casa Sollievo della Sofferenza.' There were ' ups and downs ' and many changes of luck. There were happy times, sometimes less than happy ones, often odd but almost always exceptional! In the center of the drama was Padre Pio and, at his side like a shadow, the doctor from Parma.

He is a doctor and a missionary—for on the Gargano and in Puglie we are in missionary territory. He is a businessman and head of the administration which has the responsibility of the hundreds of laborers who are working under the direction of Angelo Lupi, who is not an engineer, but will receive an honorary degree with the termination of the building. *

Who keeps alive the contacts with the 'high' Roman world as well as with the modest Pugliese world? Who approaches, with dignity and prestige the high luminaries of the scientific and medical world who come to San Giovanni Rotondo? With whom does Padre Pio confide his suffering caused by those five bleeding wounds in his hands, feet and side? With him!

He knows he has near him a doctor, and a friend, and with him he proceeds until death knocks

---

* Lupi, whom everyone thought to be an engineer but who was discovered later to have little more than an 8th grade education, was chosen by Padre Pio for this work. At the end of the construction project, he was called into court for presenting himself as an engineer, but it was impossible to accuse him of not knowing how to do that which he had already done so beautifully. Comedies of San Giovanni Rotondo!

unexpectaby at the door. The earthly cycle of the doctor, brother of Padre Pio, had its conclusion on September 7, 1954.

If I am remembering this, it is because concluded it is not. For us Guglielmo Sanguinetti is still alive as he is (probably even more so) for Padre Pio."

# A Healing Sacramental

In the very first years that I went to San Giovanni Rotondo, when everything was rustic and there were no lights along the rocky, dusty road, and the great marble hospital was still in the " dream " and " let us hope " stage with the wooden scaffolding just beginning to rise on high, I was afflicted one summer with a very disturbing intestinal condition.

The local restaurants were provided with certain dishes, mostly very greasy, to say the least. No one seemed to have heard of a cup of tea. At the moment they were all out of rice. I have a special aversion to medicine and had not brought anything of this sort with me. I met Dr. Sanguinetti along the road and asked him for help, for some remedy. He wrote a few lines on a piece of paper telling me to present it to a certain person who could be found on the ground floor of the future hospital where, in a little, half-finished room a few medicines were kept. I hurried up there but to no avail. The man in question was nowhere to be found. The door to the medicine room was locked and Dr. Sanguinetti, too, had disappeared. Despairingly, armed with a lemon, I went up to the convent to the well in the little courtyard. I had seen all the pilgrims come and go with bottles of this water, saying it was blessed. I found a glass and, filling it, added the lemon juice. After drinking it, recovery was immediate. This made me decide to bring some of this water home. Having filled a bottle, I sent it up to Padre Pio for another blessing, which was given.

At that time, I had begun to help the women who cleaned the little church. The next afternoon, after the cleaning hour terminated, I forgot the bottle hidden in a corner of the altar of St. Francis. That day, being a special feast day, there was Benediction in the afternoon, presided over by Padre Pio. So my water received the really great blessing from Our Divine Lord held in Padre Pio's hands. After Benediction, having recovered my bottle, I found myself, by chance, with it in hand when Padre Pio passed in the narrow corridor of the convent. There were a number of people crowded together. I stood silently, holding my bottle. As Padre Pio passed he stopped, looked at the bottle, and deliberately blessed it again. Home I went with my bottle of triply-blessed water and how many graces I have obtained with it! I have never let it dry— adding to it other blessed water and water from the grotto of the Archangel Michael. I will cite only two examples of the graces received with it because they somehow seem related, are of a very concrete nature, and I am absolutely convinced of their authenticity since one of the persons helped was myself, and the other, the son of a doctor—good family friends as well as neighbors.

Living in a little Riviera town, the chief summer occupation, or let us say recreation, consists in going to the seashore, to the beach. I have always enjoyed swimming and had the habit of wetting and submerging my head in the water. It seems that, about 1952, my ears suffered in some way from being filled and refilled with too much sea water. At least I attribute the cause to this; I have no real proof, however. At any rate, all that autumn and winter, one ear was afflicted with a water-like liquid which emerged from it. There was no pain but it was very annoying, especially at night when, just as I was going to sleep or during later hours, I would be awakened by a " gloo-gloo " sound and, out of the ear into the pillow would pour this water-like liquid.

Having no pain, and a natural aversion to having my ears tinkered with, I visited no doctor, contenting myself with trying an occasional remedy given me by my cousin, a pharmacist.

In the spring, this condition suddenly took a turn for the worse. Not only did it commence to become a bit painful, with the liquid increasing in quantity, but my hearing began to be impaired and the second ear was also affected. " Well, my dear," I said to myself, " the gong has sounded. You will simply have to take the train to the city and go to a specialist before it is too late." All of this was a bit distasteful to me.

I thought of Padre Pio's holy water but felt ashamed to use it—to ask for a favor from God for such a small cross, one that could easily be supported and carried. I could not, however, seem to keep my attention from the little flask of water in the bookcase of my room. " Well," I suddenly said to myself, " the best thing to do is to let Our Lord decide."

With complete casualness, almost indifference, I took a toothpick and, adding a bit of cotton to the tip, wet it with the holy water and, blessing myself, touched the inside of each ear, saying simply, " Thy will be done."

From that moment not one drop of liquid ever emerged from either of my ears. No one was more amazed than myself at this complete and instant result asked with such abandon. The only evidence that anything had ever been wrong with my ears was an occasional piece of dry scab-like material which, for a certain time came out of the ears. This terminated, my ears returned to complete normalcy. " His will was done "—part of His marvelous, mysterious design.

Now to the second incident, that for which my good friend vouches. In February, 1953, upon my return from San Giovanni Rotondo, I was immediately informed of the serious illness of Gianmaria Mazzini, the son of our good family friend, Dr. Emmanuele Mazzini. Everyone seemed very preoccupied and distressed about the case.

From my little balcony I could see the closed shutters of Gianmaria's bedroom and, imagining all the suffering therein, my heart was heavy indeed, especially at the thought of his parents. Gianmaria was a handsome boy of about twenty—their only son.

The next morning, upon my return from Mass there seemed to be no end to the people who stopped me along the main shopping street of our little town, all repeating more or less the same words: " Have you heard?—Gianmaria Mazzini—they say there is no hope . . . . " As I rounded the corner of the street leading to our apartment, I suddenly thought of the holy water blessed by Padre Pio which had cured my ears the previous year, and I decided to bring him some. Immediately, a delicate, but decided, perfume passed under my nose. My way was indicated. Hope and joy sprang in my heart.

Upon arriving home, I immediately took a large image of my beloved Lady of Divine Grace of San Giovanni Rotondo, a small photograph of Padre Pio, and armed with the little bottle of the blessed water, I hurried to the Mazzini home.

His haggard-faced father came to greet me and gratefully accepted my three gifts, promising to pray and give his son the water in small doses as best he could. Now we will let Dr. Mazzini conclude with his own words:

" On February 17, 1953, my son Gianmaria suddendly fell sick with a temperature of 40° C. (104° F.) due to tonsil pharyngitis, accompanied by deep depression, delirium and reduced sensitivity; in brief, a very serious and preoccupying status, also because various treatments with antibiotics and serum-vaccination were of no help. Six days after the outbreak of the disease, I decided to use antidiptherial serum in view of the failure of the previous therapies and in spite of the fact that laboratory analysis of tonsil secretion was negative. But even this new treatment, used in strong doses, gave negative results. The day after, Miss Clarice Bruno, having been informed of the grave illness of my son, came to visit us bringing a small bottle of the holy water which had been blessed by Padre Pio. I immediately gave it to my son who drank it by spoonfuls, according to directions. During the night, between the sixth and seventh day, my son went through a tremendous crisis and his perspiration was such that I was obliged to change all bed sheets six consecutive times, after which the temperature suddenly disappeared while the necrotic plaques adherred to his tonsils were completely detached and he was pervaded with a sense of well-being which made him mumble the following (exact) words: 'BECAUSE OF THIS FRESH AND PERFUMED AIR, I AM COMING BACK TO LIFE.' We had insistently prayed for the patient's recovery and I had approached Padre Pio to obtain his intercession. God listened to our prayers and fulfilled them."

This young man and his family spoke for years of the fresh mountain air and perfumes miraculously breathed that night—the night of the son's sudden, almost instant recovery.

# Bankers' Account - 1966

I think of this as my " Bankers' Story " because it was told to us by a family friend, a banker here in Chiavari to whom it was recounted by the president of a large bank in an important city, whom our friend knows very well.

It seems that this latter banker had a handsome only son who, at the age of twenty-six years, armed with a law degree, had decided he wanted to become a Capuchin monk. This announcement evidently had on his parents, all the quieting effects of an atomic bomb! Everything was done to discourage him, but all to no avail. The father even had recourse to the Cardinal of his city in the hope of finding some way to change the state of things, but the only help he obtained was His Eminence's promise to see that the boy would be sent to the most rugged, ancient, uncomfortable novitiate possible, saying that if he persisted under the circumstances of such penance, there could be no doubt as to his vocation, his true religious calling. So the young man was shipped off to an antiquated, damp seminary on a hilltop while the father sat at home hopefully waiting, but month after month passed and nothing happened. The banker could think of no other door at which to knock that might open the way to a new solution to the present state of affairs.

Often he unburdened himself, discussing his sorrowful state of mind with a countess, a family friend, who had a somewhat similar problem that saddened her. She too had an only son who wanted to join the Franciscan order —become a monk—to which decision she also was opposed but, due to his extremely poor eyesight he had been rejected by the religious order.

She, of course, desired her son to regain his eyesight, but not so as to become a monk. However, all the eye specialists he consulted refused to operate, saying the operation was too delicate and risky, and might not only endanger the bit of sight he had, but his life as well.

And so all these parents were, let us say, " up a tree." I am not cognizant of what facts led the countess to try Padre Pio as a last resort for the grace of her son's eyesight, but in discussing this decision with her friend the banker, she persuaded him to accompany her, saying he had nothing to lose and that Padre Pio might say his boy had no real vocation, or that since he was an only child it was his duty to remain with his parents, etc. etc.

With enormous difficulty they managed to obtain a three-minute appointment with Padre Pio immediately following his five o'clock mass. I do not know as to the countess, but the banker had never before seen or accosted Padre Pio. Now they found themselves in the cold grey dawn of the designated day, in a modest little parlor of the convent, waiting Padre Pio's entrance.

It is really very humorous to hear the bewildered banker's description of the scene. Finally, he says, a door opens and an old monk arrives. He has a white beard and can scarcely walk and is supported on either side by a younger member of his order—Padre Pio.

He looks at them with his great, penetrating eyes. After kissing his half-gloved hand, the countess hastens to plead her son's cause: the question of his eyesight, saying the doctors refuse to operate because he is considered practically inoperable. " Who said he is inoperable? " says Padre Pio. " Operate, he will see perfectly! "

Extremely happy at hearing these words, the countess begins to worry about the second part of her problem— that if her son can see, he will be accepted into the Franciscan order. " Padre," she implores, " our son would want to become a monk, but he is our only child."

" Oh no! " says Padre Pio. " You have another child, a daughter." " Oh, yes," answers the bewildered countess, " But she has been married for almost twelve years and for congenital reasons can have no children. We have no heirs, no grandchildren."

" Who says she can have no children?," queries Padre Pio. " Partorira! " (" She will give birth.") " But your son must become a monk." The interview begins to draw to an end; his young assistants move Padre Pio towards the door. The banker is flabbergasted and silent—he has lost his tongue, but he has since found it again to repeat his story over and over again to our banker friend who, in turn, repeats it over and over to his friends.

Oh, yes! I am forgetting to add that within a year the countess' son was operated on and regained his eyesight, and his sister, after twelve years of marriage, gave birth to her first child!

And the banker's son stuck it out on his hilltop and in the year 1966 offered his first Mass. Since he already had degrees, knew Latin and Greek and had a good religious education, he only had to study two years before receiving Holy Orders. The last I heard, he was thinking of becoming a missionary in South America.

The bankers shake their head mystified ... it just doesn't add up in the books ... ! But they and their friends have begun to learn that God has his own way of keeping books!

# ANGELIC WORLD

# Grotto of St, Michael the Archangel

To the frequent visitor to San Giovanni Rotondo who has the opportunity of accosting Padre Pio in and out of the confessional, it is almost impossible not to conclude, one time or another, that it is not by chance that Divine Providence has placed Padre Pio so near to Monte Sant'Angelo and the famous basilica-grotto of St. Michael the Archangel,* for although almost forgotten and ignored by the fast moving modern world, " this is the most ancient, venerated basilica dedicated to angelic devotion " (490 A. D.) and in the past Popes, Bishops, Emperors and Princes formed a constant part of the procession of pilgrims from all parts of the world who journeyed against terrific odds and difficulties (1000 meters above sea level) to visit the celebrated grotto so that the Gargano, writes Baronio, " became the source of an infinite number of extraordinary graces for Christians, and even today fortunate is he who visits the sacred grotto and places himself under the most loving protection of the prince of angels, St. Michael. " This is the only Catholic church not consecrated by human hand, and contains the only altar without the usual

* Thirty five miles to be exact.

blessed stone because, in one of his apparitions, the Archangel pronounced the grotto already consecrated, and left the imprint of his foot in the stone altar.

The story of the many apparitions and the history of this grotto church are really much too fascinating and profound to be touched upon too briefly, and inadequately, in an article such as this. Let us simply say that Padre Pio, with his great devotion to St. Michael, is truly an instrument in the hands of God to lead thousands of pilgrims again to this mystic grotto, and so rediscover with new freshness this great archangel, and with him the whole angelic world.

With good reason this province has for centuries borne the name of the " Angelic Gargano," and it is impossible not to observe how this primitive and poor little city of perhaps thirty thousand souls seems to have been deliberately cut off from the world of today, left in its simplicity to form a sort of spiritual oasis for us poor humans, so engulfed, and at times almost suffocated by the materialistic desert in which we live and move.

Here past and present become fused, and already on the tortuous, timeworn, eighty-eight steps that lead to the sanctuary below, one can almost feel the presence of the generations of pilgrims who have hallowed with their penance and prayer this holy basilica.

As to Daisy and me, on our first visit (of consecration) all I can say is that we became smitten, immediately enamored of, and devoted to this sacred spot. We had not expected to find, in this remote village, such a cargo of archaeological and artistic treasure. But the greatest treasure we found was St. Michael the Archangel and the great door he opened on the whole angelic world—a world of friends, not new it is true, but become suddenly vital, concrete, alive. We had almost forgotten that our religion teaches us that after the Virgin Mary, St. Michael is the highest of celestial figures, above all other creatures and saints.

## A Potent Ally

It is about the year 1957. It is Padre Pio's confessional hour and the little church is filled with people. Although separated by several yards, I am standing directly in front of his confessional and able to see him very clearly. A charming, well-dressed young woman emerges from her confession in tears. We have never met but, for some reason, she passes through all the people and comes directly to me. She weeps upon my shoulder, confiding that Padre Pio has denied her absolution. In her hand she holds a crucifix that she had brought for him to bless. She seems a fine sort of person. I do not know what to say being ignorant of what her confession has involved. Padre Pio keeps gazing fixedly at us. I feel that he wants us to understand something but I am helpless.

Finally, she confides, " I only said that sometimes I had impure thoughts " and he said, " Do you cast them from you immediately? " I answered, " Padre, sometimes I am unable to do so instantly." Then he replied, " For only one deliberate sin of thought was the great angel Lucifer cast out of heaven. " And, so saying, he concluded the confession without giving me absolution." I try to console her and I continue to look into Padre Pio's eyes. What is it that he wants?

Suddenly I get an idea. " Have you been to the grotto of St. Michael the Archangel? " " No," she replies, " I have been here ten days, and although it was in the program to go, I never got there. Now in an hour or so I must catch the bus for my train to Milan."

" I think that perhaps Padre Pio would like us to understand that what weakly and humanly speaking we find great difficulty in doing alone, we can do much better with St. Michael's protection and assistance. He is the Angelic Warrior who combats evil, helping us to keep in subjection to spirit and will the numerous variety of human passions that are always seeking to get the upper hand, and by dominating the individual end up also by dominating society."

She looks at me hopefully. She will inquire if this is what Padre Pio wants.

The next morning, I see her about to board her bus. She comes running to me, embraces me with affection and joy. " You were right! I went to another monk and enquired. He agreed and I postponed my departure and went to the grotto to place myself under St. Michael's protection. Oh, thank you—and good-bye! "

Little things but with great significance that happen at San Giovanni Rotondo.

For those who although separated physically from this sanctuary, but who, feeling it spiritually near, are desirous of consecrating, placing themselves under the particular protection of St. Michael the Archangel, as Padre Pio desires, we print the prayer recited for this occasion. Obligation? The recital daily of a prayer, or ejaculation to St. Michael—a spontaneous prayer—even consisting of but two or three words such as " St. Michael protect me," or " St. Michael defend me. "

*Prayer to St. Michael the Archangel*
*Act of Consecration*

*Oh most Noble Prince of the Angelic Hierarchies, valorous warrior of Almighty God and zealous lover of His glory, terror of the rebellious angels, and love and delight of all the just ones, my beloved Archangel St. Michael, I, today offer and consecrate myself to you, and place myself, my family, and all I possess under your most powerful protection.*
*I entreat you not to look at how little I, as your servant have to offer, being only a wretched sinner, but to gaze rather, with favorable eye at the heartfelt affection with which this offering is made and remember that, if from this day onward I am under your patronage, you must during all my life assist me, and procure for me the pardon of my many grievous offenses and sins, the grace to love with all my heart my God, my dear Saviour Jesus, and my sweet Mother Mary, and obtain for*

*me all the help necessary to arrive at my crown of glory.*

*Defend me always from my spiritual enemies, particularly in the last moments of my life.*

*Come then, oh Glorious Prince, and succour me in my last struggle, and with your powerful weapon cast far from me into the infernal abyss that prevaricator and proud angel that one day you prostrated in the celestial battle.*

*Our Father, Hail Mary, and Glory Be . . .*

*St. Michael defend us in our daily battle so that we may not perish in the last judgment.*

" Let us raise on high the standard of St. Michael. "

Pope Pius XII.

" Maybe the time will come when Satan will be recognized as Satan, and the Archangel will assume once more his mission of anti-materialism, and the Gargano will become the Sanctuary of civilization and of virtue. "

(L'Osservatore Romano, 1948)

# Guardian Angel

> " Remember that God is inside of us when we
> are in the state of His grace, and outside of us
> when we are in grievous sin. But His angel never
> abandons us. He is our most sincere and trusted
> friend even when, through our fault, we sadden
> him with our bad behavior. "

Padre Pio

If we have already observed that it would seem a
design of Divine Providence that Padre Pio should have
been placed so close to the grotto basilica of St. Michael
the Archangel, one of the factors in leading to this
conclusion is his constant allusion to the angelic world.
Angels form part of his everyday conversation, both in
and out of the confessional. Not only in bidding farewell
to some pilgrim will he use phrases such as " May the
angel of God accompany you," " May the angel of God
open for you closed doors." " May the angel of God be
for you light, help, strength, comfort, and guidance,"
but in confession he often tells penitents to send him
their angels when in need. To one of my friends who
lamented the distance that separated them when a difficult decision had to be made, he said, " Send me your

angel," whereupon to her answer, " But Padre, do you listen to him? " came the reply, " And do you think I am deaf?! " These words are not used humorously or lightly; but in complete sincerity and simplicity.

One woman to whom he advised sending her angel, did so on the occasion of one of his anniversaries. A few days later, she received a letter from a person who lived in San Giovanni Rotondo who, in confession had been told by Padre Pio to write her saying " the Padre thanks you for your spiritual greetings."

In a book entitled " L'Angelo di Dio " by G. P. Siena, we read of a lawyer by the name of Attilio De Sanctis, who lived in Fano (Provincia of Pesaro) who was completely mystified by the fact that he had driven his car for twenty-seven miles while fast asleep, without accident. On a visit to San Giovanni Rotondo, he had the good fortune to encounter Padre Pio in a corridor, together with another person and, upon inquiring as to what had happened that night, he received the calm answer, " You fell asleep and your guardian angel drove your car."

Really not so extraordinary as would seem when we consider that the angels obey God's orders and, if that day God so willed, who are we to question?

The many accounts of Padre Pio and the angels could fill a book by themselves. In a sense, how could it be otherwise when he, as a son of St. Francis of Assisi cannot help but live immersed in the Gospels whose pages repeatedly speak of angels?

But two examples: an angel appeared in dreams to St. Joseph the first time to exhort him to leave for Egypt with the Holy Child and His mother; the second

148

time to counsel him to return to Israel since those who wanted the life of the child were now dead. (Matt. 2: 13-19)

I personally do thank Padre Pio from the bottom of my heart for making me aware of this concrete angelic friendship from which I have derived constant benefit and assistance in needy moments.

" To His angels He has given for you this command—to protect you in all your roads; they will carry you on their hands in order that your foot may not stumble on the rocks " (Ps. 91: 11-12)

# THE DEVIL

It is not pleasant to interrupt our talk of angels to speak of their exact opposite—Satan, and yet it is impossible to speak of one without speaking of the other, both belonging to the same spiritual world that has dropped from the thoughts and convictions of a great number of minds today. It has become all too common to speak of angels in a purely symbolic role, and the devil as a mere negation of good, not as real creatures.

I must write of this, albeit poorly and inefficiently, because it is one of the messages Padre Pio keeps repeating and sending us: " Never has the devil found such fertile territory upon which to work as in this era when his very existence is denied by so many."

None other than Andrè Gide admits, " While we cannot serve God if we do not believe in Him, on the other hand, the devil has no need of our belief in him. In fact, never is he so well served as when denied or ignored by us."

St. Peter says: " Your enemy the devil is prowling around like a roaring lion, looking for someone to eat " (1 Peter: 5-9)

From the booklet, " A Few Brief Notes on Padre Pio " by Father Rosset, which carries an Imprimatur, under the heading, "Has Padre Pio Special Devotions?," we read: "Apart from the Passion of Our Lord, he has a predilection for Our Lady and St. Michael the Archangel, and he exhorts all to these devotions. Padre Pio emphasizes the fact that St. Michael is our protector against the inevitable snares of the devil.

It may be of interest to note that Padre Pio is sometimes visited by the devil in revenge for having snatched souls from damnation. The devil mistreats him physically and his very life would be in danger were he not protected by a higher power.

One day in August, 1964, Padre Pio did not celebrate Mass and admitted to diabolic cause his blackened eye and head bruises. From his earliest years Padre Pio has been tormented and tried diabolically in every way imaginable, spiritually and materially. There is very little Padre Pio could not tell us of the devil and his machinations."

I am going to present to the reader two stories in this regard because I know them to be genuine and of our times, even though many will want to classify them as medieval and outdated, as though certain truths went up and down like women's skirts. The first one, entitled "The Devil, Cruel and Vindictive," is written by Padre Emilio, whom I personally know, and is in a simple style due to the fact that it appeared in the monthly bulletin "I Fratini" (June, 1967,) which is dedicated to the seminary vocations of the Capuchin order of Foggia!

# THE DEVIL, CRUEL AND VINDICTIVE

" Long ago, in 1917, I was a " fratino " (a young seminary student of the Capuchin order in the convent of San Giovanni Rotondo), together with perhaps fifteen or so other boys. Our superiors were Padre Paolino, the Superior, from Casacalenda, who taught us, and Padre Pio, our Spiritual Director and confessor.

We slept in a dormitory, composed of two large communicating rooms and situated in front of Padre Pio's cell. Padre Pio slept with us in the first of these two rooms, that is, with two other boys and myself. Padre Pio's bed was placed in the right-hand corner of the room, facing the entrance, and was hidden by two pieces of white cloth that served as curtains. These hung from sturdy iron bars that were well planted in the wall and that were supported and joined by another strong iron bar that stood upright, column-fashion, and which in turn emerged from a heavy iron pedestal on the floor.

One night we all heard strange noises of iron bars banging and echoing, and producing such a frightening confusion of sounds as to be comparable only to that which is audible when a train is traveling at high speed through an underground tunnel.
None of us moved or cried out from fright, but we felt safe only when curled up, head and all, under the blankets of our little beds. In the morn-

ing, however, we found our dear Padre Spiritual Director sitting on the corner of his bed appearing very fatigued and worn out. The iron bars that had sustained his curtain were on the floor, twisted and bent in a manner that terrified everyone because only a giant could have had the strength to produce such a result with his own two hands. Our fright and curiosity brought us immediately to the side of our dear Padre, to ask him what had happened. He did not in any way lose his composure and answered very simply, " Let us go to the choir and pray because our dear Lord is so good."

A few days later we learned from him that it had been the devil who had beaten him and worked such havoc with the iron bars about his bed. And do you know why? Because, with his prayers, Padre Pio was sustaining and protecting a " fratino " who slept in the adjoining room to resist a very strong temptation and to conserve his purity.

The iron bars were fixed and straightened the same day by heavy hammer blows, by a man bearing the name of Vincenzino, an old-time miller from San Giovanni Rotondo." *

---

* Copied and translated from " I Fratini " (January 1967,) a monthly bulletin dedicated to the seminary vocations of the Capuchin order of Foggia.

# *Witness in the night*

It was an autumn evening at San Giovanni Rotondo. At this time our pensione entrance, and dining room, were still " all in one " but meals had already begun to be served family style, the guests seated around one large table. Having finished the evening meal, some of us still lingered together chatting and enjoying the bit of warmth that emerged from the terra-cotta, woodburning stove in the corner. The door suddenly opened and from behind the heavy, padded curtains that hung before it, protecting diners from the cold blasts of air, emerged the blue-gray clad figure of a young aviation officer of perhaps twenty-eight years of age.

He was not one of the group stopping at the pensione at the time and, at that hour—about ten o'clock—when most persons in the vicinity had already retired for the night in order to get some sleep before the four o'clock rising hour, one did not expect visitors or social calls.

Conversation ceased as all eyes fixed themselves inquiringly in his direction. After a subdued " Good evening," he asked permission to seat himself at the table with us. The permission was readily granted.

He told us that he was going from pensione to pensione, from a sense of spiritual duty—of obligation—to recount what he had witnessed with his own two eyes that very day, and would like also to tell us.

He said that on this, his brief visit at San Giovanni Rotondo, he had gone with a busload of pilgrims (I don't know what part of Italy they came from) to the grotto of St. Michael the Archangel. If I remember correctly, he was not a part of the group but had taken advantage of their invitation to join this round-trip excursion.

Once in the grotto church, while the group was gathered up front about the main altar and the statue of St. Michael, about their own business and prayers, he had stopped almost at the entrance of the church at the little office desk to buy some souvenir medals and images connected with the grotto. He thus had his back turned toward the others and was interested in his own affairs and the purchases he was selecting.

Immediately to his right, raised only two or three steps above the level of the church, was the old " coro " (choir) with its dark, carved, wooden seats and great windows and balcony opening on the luminous valley below.

He said that all at once he heard a terrifying scream of howling nature emerge from the group up front. Before he had time to turn to see what had happened, very close to him, there passed, running toward the choir balcony to precipitate and disappear from sight into the valley below, the most horrible, monstrous looking creature that he had ever seen. From what I gathered, a sort of mixture of man and beast in appearance, and yet neither. A short, dark, horrible thing which ran furiously from the angelic altar up front.

He later was told that one of the pilgrim group had been brought by his friends to the grotto, a so-called possessed-by-the-devil person in whom the modern world (into which category I imagine this young officer fell) does not believe.

I don't know what prayer had been formulated for him before the altar of St. Michael, the great enemy of Satan, but St. Michael had acted. Again he had won his battle and the sufferer had been liberated. The wings on this young officer's uniform bore truthfully a new significance that night. He had found his spiritual wings, and with great humility and apostolic fervor, he went tirelessly from pensione to pensione, to " bear witness " with dignified calm and firm decision.

I wish, dear reader, that I could tell you more of this young man—who he is, where he is, what his life has been since he disappeared again into the night, just as he had come. Maybe we shall find him again, as so many others who have been woven together in this— God's pattern, at San Giovanni Rotondo.

After reading these two accounts many of us may experience a moment of perplexity wondering why the devil, belonging as he does to the spirit world, and so specialized in tempting us in more than subtle manner, has been presented to us in such physical and ugly form. Could it be that, in this intellectually proud, and yet materialistic age, a materialistic vision of Satan is a form of convincing argument conceded by a merciful God observant of our needs? And, that stripping from him the illusive veiling with which he is wont to transform himself to worldly eyes, we have been able to see him as he truly is, the incarnation of all that is distorted, ugly and depraved?

As to Padre Pio being physically tormented by the devil, perhaps this, too, can be put in the above category, that is, a demonstration permitted by God for our benefit, with some persons adding the plausible explanation that Padre Pio having so early in life arrived at a matured saintliness, overcoming already in his youth the majority of the trying temptations and spiritual torments to which we are still so subject, this is another form of " battle "—of paying with his sacrifice for the conversions and graces which come to us through his intercession and prayers.

All we can do is hazard a few thoughts on the subject, for never will we small creatures be able to measure the designs of an infinitely loving (and how wise!) God with a purely human yardstick.

Padre Pio, in speaking of Satan, tells us:

" The temptations, confusions, and torments are the offerings of our enemy. Remember this: if the devil is creating a great confusion around you, he is still *outside* of you and not *inside*. That which should hold terror for us is his calm complacent union with the human soul."

" The devil is like a mad dog tied by a chain. Beyond the length of the chain he cannot catch hold of anyone. And you, therefore, keep your distance. If you get too close you will be caught. Remember, the devil has only one door with which to enter into our soul—our will. There are no secret or hidden doors. No sin is a true sin if we have not wilfully consented."

"Let us always remain closely united to the Holy Spirit and to prudence, for the devil hovers close to the soul of the foolish."

In conclusion a few "bits" translated here, and there from an article by Padre Michelangelo, a famous preacher, that appeared but recently in the monthly bulletin "Casa Sollievo della Sofferenza."

... "Pope Paul in closing the year of "faith" (1967) in reciting in St. Peter's square his "Credo" for all the world, included the angels.

... "I believe in the existence of the angels"

... "This is therefore an important ecclesiastical document; but we brethern, have the Holy Scriptures. In the Holy Scriptures we read constantly of the angels ... as well as of Satan. He is always present, and should we deny the existence of Satan we should be obliged to deny the Gospels, ... Satan is a fallen angel and conserves the nature, and power of the angelic nature.

... Saint Michael archangel was famous in the old testament ... but made his first appearance after the new testament in the year 400 AD at Monte Sant'Angelo in the Gargano, and the eyes of the whole Christian world were focused upon this grotto ....

The Gargano has been, and remains the Gospel of the Angels. One cannot speak of the angels ignoring Monte Sant'Angelo, or ignoring the Gargano.

Was this, my brethern, perhaps a prelude to that which was to happen later with the presence on the Gargano of our dear Padre Pio? ...

Padre has been, and is, I might say the modern Gospel

on the angels . . . . To all his spiritual sons and daughters, he has always spoken constantly of the angels . . . .

It pleases me to conclude these words on the angelic world with a remembrance regarding a series of sermons I preached during the months of May and June, 1956, at San Giovanni Rotondo. Each week I spoke of a different subject. The first week I spoke of " hope," the second week of " faith " etc. Finally I dedicated a week to the argument of " temptation; " therefore I had to speak of Satan, the existence of Satan, the nature of Satan, the " force " of Satan, the " weakness " of Satan, the " action of Satan " etc. On the Wednesday of this week my theme was the " nature " of Satan.

I began, like St. Thomas, by saying what Satan is not. Some, I said " say that Satan is the world, that Satan is the battle between good and evil, that Satan is propaganda, is science etc.

I spoke of the various wordly opinions regarding Satan, that is, that Satan does not exist.

After which I said that which Satan truly is according to Holy Scripture. It seemed to me to have spoken very well.

(I do remember that that particular evening a large number of pilgrims arrived, crowding the little church. But with their buses waiting, and their minutes counted they were obliged to leave before the termination of the sermon).

After the Sermon and Benediction many visitors filled the old sacristy, and Padre Pio, upon returning had a word for all, including myself, with whom he often joked.

Suddenly he turned to me and before all this group asked " And who ever taught you how to preach? "

" Well," I replied " no one taught me; the little I know I picked up by myself." " But does this seem to you the way to preach? "

" Padre I don't know. I do what I can. You tell me how I can do better."

Padre Pio continued " What a way to preach! You begin by saying that which the devil is not. That the devil does not exist, that the devil is the world etc. You lose so much time in saying that which he is not, that half the people have left the church before you begin saying that which he truly is. Does this seem a good way of preaching? "

" Tell me Padre."

" Do you want me to tell you? First one should begin by saying that which the devil is, that is, that which God has revealed us in Holy Scripture, in the Gospels. The devil is this, and this, and this . . . . "

Perhaps Padre Pio was thinking of the beatings received from the devil, of the battles the devil had waged with him. Therefore Padre Pio knew only too well that the devil is not " public opinion " nor " the world."

How thoroughly he had experienced what Satan is!

" First you begin by saying what Satan is. Then if you still have time you can add. " There are some stupid ones in the world who maintain that he does not exist, or who insist that he is such and such a thing. The devil however etc. etc. etc."

" Padre Pio thank you. Another time I shall remember. I had learned from St. Thomas to use this method."

" St. Thomas, or not, . . . first one says that which God has said, and then afterwards that which man has said." And so I have done in all my successive sermons."

" Souls are not given to us as gifts; they must be purchased. Let us not forget how dearly they cost Jesus. Now, as always they must be paid for with the same coin." Padre Pio.

*OTHER STORIES*

# American at San Giovanni Rotondo

June, 1967: On the road at San Giovanni Rotondo, I am introduced to a Chicagoan (Forest Park, Ill.) A big, squarecut man with good, honest eyes. He has just arrived from the States, hopes to have a long-merited vacation, to pass the winter with his wife and relatives in Fara San Martino Chieti, his birthplace. His name is Angelo Salvitti.

I have seen him in prayer in church. He looks neither to right nor left, but kneels with profound sincerity and great humility and prays. This is his story told in his own brief words:

" In 1945 I became ill with acute bleeding colitis. It was so bad that it required hospitalization (about eight weeks at Hines Veterans' Hospital,) and from that period until 1953 I was continuously hospitalized—approximately one month in, one month out. Hemorrhages varied from seven to thirty-five daily. In 1950 when I was hospitalized, I asked for a weekend pass to go home. This I obtained. On the Sunday morning of this weekend I went to Mass. At the beginning of the Mass, Father Carty (author of the book on Padre Pio,) announced that in the evening in the church basement, there would be a lecture and slide presentation, on Padre Pio. I attended. My heart responded to the lecture instantly and I felt a great faith in Padre Pio.

I began immediately to pray to God to give me the strength to work sufficiently to be able to put aside enough money to pay for a trip to Italy in order to go and see Padre Pio. God was good and granted my request.

Now, my former employer, Charles Ross (Economy Plumbing and Heating Company, Skokie, Illinois,) as well as my fellow workers, confess that, due to my condition, they did not think I would ever reach Italy alive. Upon landing, I went first to my home-town to see my aged father. Among other friends of my childhood days I met again a woman by the name of Filomena Cipola who was devoted to Padre Pio. She gave me a letter of introduction to Nicolino Coccomazzi of San Giovanni Rotondo, asking him to find a room for me.

I arrived about six o'clock in the evening. I found him without difficulty and presented my letter which I later learned also contained some details regarding my illness.

Leaving my wife and sister in their room at San Giovanni Rotondo, Nicolino took me immediately up to the Capuchin convent where Padre Pio was. I did not dream I was going to see Padre Pio that evening, thinking I was simply going to sign up for my confession turn.

Imagine my surprise when, in the dark November evening, upon arriving and ringing a little bell to which a rope was attached, the small convent door was opened by a monk who admitted us and disappeared. I was greeted by a wonderful wave of perfume but still did not understand what was happening. Without a word, Nicolino took me upstairs to a cell door over which was inscribed " No. 5." Nicolino knocked on the door and a powerful voice inside said " Avanti." We entered, and I was stunned to find myself suddenly in Padre Pio's presence. I will never forget those great dark eyes as they looked at me. I lost my tongue.

Nicolino, kneeling down and kissing Padre Pio's stigmatized hand,* said: ' This man has come from America to see you, Padre.' As I in turn knelt before him, he himself offered me his hand and, with the other patted my head caressingly and said, ' Bravo, Bravo. Iddio ti benedice, figlio mio.' (' Bravo, bravo. God blesses you, my son.') As he said those words the burning pain that I had carried in my abdominal region for so many years disappeared completely and has never more returned and never again have I had a hemorrhage and since that moment, I have been able to eat and drink anything I desire.

* This practice is still in common use in Italy. The gesture indicates a reverence for the priesthood and the hand that consecrates the Divine Host at Mass.

As I have already said, this encounter left me speechless and I did not ask for anything regarding my illness. Nicolino, having observed my silence, went himself the following morning to Padre Pio to ask him to pray for my illness. Padre Pio answered, " Tell him he is well now and to eat and drink anything he desires. I HAVE ALREADY BEEN PRAYING FOR HIM FOR A LONG TIME! "

# Anna Maria

In the very first years of my trips to San Giovanni Rotondo, Anna Maria's mother who lives in another town, comes to see me in a desolate state of mind. Anna Maria, age nine, suffers from convulsions (perhaps epilepsy, I do not know.) She is under the care of a well-known nerve specialist who, having failed to obtain results from the treatment prescribed, had decided to operate on the child's brain. Will I recommend her to Padre Pio's intercession? After much discussion and despite the length and difficulty of the trip, it is decided that Anna Maria will accompany us to San Giovanni Rotondo. So off we go in a crowded after-the-war train, in the hot month of August (the Italian vacation month,) traveling all the way to Rome—seven hours—standing in the corridor or sitting for a bit on the edge of our suitcases.

In Rome we have a five-hour wait before leaving at midnight for Foggia and we think ourselves fortunate to find three hard wooden seats on the train upon which to spend the remainder of the night.

At San Giovanni Rotondo each morning at the dawn hour, we drag a reluctant, drowsy Anna Maria from her bed, still under the effects of the sedative medicine she has taken the night before. We bring her with us to

Mass and keep her fasting, without her very necessary morning medicines, so that she can receive Holy Communion from Padre Pio's hands at nine-thirty. As our confession day begins to draw near, we compose a letter asking Padre Pio to implore Anna Maria's cure from Our Lady of Divine Grace.

The morning after the letter is given to him, as the three of us kneel together on the altar steps to receive Holy Communion from his hands, he stops suddenly and looks back after communicating us, staring fixedly at Anna Maria. In his fingers he holds high, without moving, the Divine Host he has been in the act of giving to another person. In that instant, I feel something wonderful has happened, as though through that Host our dear Lord has spoken to him—has spoken to him of AnnaMaria. Seeing his great eyes look so intently at her, I am overjoyed, and certain the grace has been obtained.

The next day, our confession turn arrives and so we instruct our little pigtailed Anna Maria to ask at the end of her confession: " Padre, my mother would like to know what I must do in order to get better, to recover " (guarire.) Upon hearing these words, Padre Pio begins to laugh: " Ah—e me lo chiedi a me? Basta pregare! " (" Oh—and you are asking me? Just pray! Prayer is enough.") Of course, her mother, still anxious, implores his prayers, and she gives an offering for Padre Pio's hospital, but more important, from that day onward, they begin reciting a rosary together, family-style, husband and aunt included, each night before going to bed. Anna Maria has never had another attack, or medical visit connected with this disturbance.

A year later, however, the family begins wondering what may be physically happening inside the child's head (brain,) and comes to ask my opinion about having a brain examination (something like an electro-encephalogram) made of Anna Maria's head. " Remember," I reply, " Padre Pio says ' Basta pregare ' (' Prayer is enough,') and you have prayed and Anna Maria has never suffered another attack despite the fact that she has never again taken her morning medicine. So as not to lack in faith, why don't you at least ask Padre Pio's opinion? "

So Anna Maria's aunt joins me in my projected trip to San Giovanni Rotondo, and arrived, we lose no time in sending our query to Padre Pio. Our answer is: " Non svegliate il cane che dorme." (" Do not awaken a sleeping dog.") No electro-encephalogram is made of Anna Maria's brain. Another year passes, and Anna Maria continues her normal, going to school life, with no attacks. However, even though the morning medicine had been eliminated since our original San Giovanni Rotondo trip, the night medicine has been administered in reduced doses. There is some indecision as to whether or not it should be stopped altogether and so Anna Maria's aunt once again goes to ask Padre Pio's counsel.

In confession she presents her query. " Oh," he replies brusquely, as he so often does when he wants to hide a grace obtained through his prayers and sufferings, " and if you continue giving her the habit of these sedatives, what will she take years from now if for some reason or other she should have need of them? "

The medicine is discontinued and years have passed with never a recurrence of the malady. Anna Maria is grown-up and walks her way happily, a successful young school teacher knowing, probably, only part of her story.

# PILGRIM'S PROGRESS

*A Broken Motor.*

The year is 1954 or 1955. Our " Prayer Group Pilgrimage " is nearing the end of its second day of arduous travel. We are almost at San Giovanni Rotondo, about 140 miles distant to be exact. It is late afternoon —open countryside with very few places of habitation— when suddendly the bus breaks down. We are, says the driver, in a " frazione " on the out-skirts of a place called Vasto. There are a few stray old houses, a bar of a sort, and fortunately a bus service-center where four or five mechanics belonging to a private bus company are stationed, at least at that moment.

Our driver is naturally very grateful that this unfortunate incident has happened where he can have efficient, fraternal help. And, naturally, so am I and the rest of the group. We all climb out, and though very tired, are not averse to stretching our legs for a while, and inhaling a breath of nice spring air. We leave the mechanics to their work and we saunter about, even though there is absolutely nothing of interest to look at, apart from the sky with its colors of the approaching sunset.

Naturally, I am under nervous tension since I am responsible for all these people stranded about in this next-to-nothing locality, and I anxiously await the

173

verdict—the diagnosis as to what is ailing the innards of our faithful and comfortable bus. The trouble seems to be in the midsection. After some to-do, it is jacked up, a strong light is placed underneath, and the inspection and consultation begins, the mechanics climbing in and out from beneath it with all the accompanying mechanical instruments needed in such operations.

Almost everyone tries to be cheerful, to comfort me, to be pleasant and take it in stride—laughing it off. We have a young priest with us as a spiritual director, a person of few words, but sensitive and generous. He does everything possible to be helpful. One hour passes, then two, then three; our driver looks very distressed. They have, he says, stripped the gears and all connecting mechanisms but have not been able to find the trouble. He has phoned his bus company at Chiavari and has been told to order another bus for us immediately. There is confusion, and phone calls are impeded by trouble with the wires. We cannot get all our local calls through, and no bus arrives.

A new part is ordered from Verona but will take forty hours to arrive. The situation is very black. There is no restaurant, or place to sleep. The so-called " bar " has yielded its utmost—a glass of vermouth. The smiles on faces are becoming a bit wan. The fourth hour comes and goes, still the same confusing scene, now bathed in moonlight. People, tired people, sitting on their suitcases, scattered in groups here and there. Close to the fifth hour, everyone is at the breaking point when a bus arrives—for us.

Hopefully I climb aboard with my young priest friend to inspect it. It is a very ugly, old, worn-down thing, much too small for our number of passengers, and has no baggage compartment. It is doubtful if the group can, standing, absolutely packed together, even find sufficient space to get in and close the doors. And what about the baggage to be left high and dry in a deserted spot?

I feel desolate and terrified. While we are considering these things, a few of the less resistant, nervous passengers climb in with their baggage. The narrow aisle becomes clogged and the passengers, hysterical. They will not listen to reason, they will not move. After this scene, what is left of me staggers out. My young priest friend keeps saying. " Porta frutto. Porta frutto."

My poor dear mother is sitting on her suitcase, still with a chipper smile on her lips as has my aunt who is standing next to her. No one can suggest anything at the moment, the pieces simply do not fit!

There we are, a pilgrimage travelling under the banner of Padre Pio's prayer group, and in the great confusion, I, at least, had not thought of praying!

In my purse, I suddenly spy a small photo of Padre Pio's stigmatized hand which I had placed there sometime before. I bring it hurriedly to our now wordless bus driver who, at the moment, is observing his colleagues still fussing in the strong illumination under the jacked-up bus.

With the few breaths that are still left in me, I say, " Please put this in your wallet and ask Padre Pio to give us a hand." " Oh," he says, " I have faith in Padre Pio; I went to visit him once a few years back when I lived near Ancona." " That is fine," I say, " but pray that he will lend us a hand, work things out the best way possible."

Not more than two or three minutes pass before our happy driver comes running to me. " Signorina, Signorina," he says, " We have found the difficulty. It is next to nothing! We can fix it up in a few minutes. Within fifteen minutes we will be on our way again."

I am too dazed to believe my ears, but it is true. In less than twenty minutes we are rolling along the moonlit road to San Giovanni Rotondo—bags, baggage and passengers all in their place.

What had been wrong? A small external repair completely visible to the eye of all—a small coupling for the clutch that no one had seen for more than five hours!

Upon our return to Chiavari, poor Mancini, (our bus driver) is not only " raked over the coals," as the saying goes, by the director of his company, but is on the verge of being discharged for having created such a scene and commotion and for being so stupid as not to see such a small, obvious repair, right under his nose.

I plead his cause; " Remember, he was not alone. None of the other mechanics was able, in five hours time, to see it either." The director shakes his head, completely mystified, he cannot believe it.

Mancini who later took us on pilgrimages to San Giovanni Rotondo on two additional occasions, and I, have our opinion on the subject. All these years have passed but the other morning when we were having a cup of coffee together and I was having him write in his own words what had been wrong with the bus so as to be precise and not reveal my ignorance of motors

176

and mechanics, he took out his wallet and showed me the photograph of Padre Pio's hand, the one of that night. He has never since moved without it; accompanying it is an image of Our Lady of Divine Grace, and another of Padre Pio's face.

He is a square-cut, sturdy man, a devoted husband and father, but he insists he is beginning to feel the passing years and that within a few more he will not be up to handling a thirty-five passenger bus on a thousand mile trip—with all the visits and stop-overs of a week's constant travel.

" Signorina," he says wistfully, " can't you organize another pilgrimage? " I would like to see Padre Pio once more. I am yearning to see him again." " Dear Mancini," I reply, " the years have passed for me too. I think ' Il Padrone' who lives above us wants me to tackle another form of activity at the present moment."

*A Broken Seat.*

Another pilgrimage! It is about three in the afternoon, the tired hour when everyone would like to doze a bit, but up front—and with a loudspeaker to boot—a couple has taken to singing. It is really quite a blast! The man is an extremely nervous person, and both are very proud of their voices.

I have already had enough to do with the gentleman to realize that there is no sufficiently diplomatic way to suggest that he even pause a while. Further back are two elderly, aristocratic women who can no longer tolerate this constant concert. Their heads are splitting and they threaten to get off the bus in the open countryside if it does not cease.

I begin to perspire: between two fires! It is time to pray!

A group of us in the back say an ardent, imploring " Salve Regina " (Hail Holy Queen.) We have no sooner finished than, up front, there is a sudden commotion.

Marisa, my witty blond friend, who has been sitting in a swivel chair next to the driver in order to assist him with the road maps, has tumbled onto the floor. Her swivel chair has decided to break down! Amid much laughter, she is picked up while others busy themselves fixing her chair. In the general merriment, the singers forget to sing: the elderly women forget their headaches. In a short time peace and calm are restored.

" Nice work," Marisa will say to me later, " your knocking the seat from under me with your ' Salve Regina. '! "

Just another coincidence, the reader will say? All I can reply is: If you are ever " up a tree," just try praying, and let some of those coincidences come to your aid. They really are very handy!

Part IV

# *FLASHES*

*Round Trip.*


1967: a member of the " Camera " (Italian House of Representatives) who, with his wife is very devoted to Padre Pio and spends, together with her, a month or so each summer at San Giovanni Rotondo, brings two important office-holding members of said Camera to Padre Pio!

After Benediction, he is able to bring them up to Padre Pio's cell. He enters, the first " Onorevole " enters, the second " Onorevole " is in the process of entering when Padre Pio says: " And you! What are you doing here? Leave! "

The Onorevole who is accustomed to deference and compliments, is quite surprised and offended. " But Padre," he hazards, " I only came to receive your blessing."

" You have already had it," replies Padre Pio. " Leave! "

He will afterward remark to his friend and guide: " If he is really a saint, I know why he had good reason to send me out. But, if it is only a bad disposition, then . . . . "

Shortly afterward, the Onorevole is in an expensive hotel in a mountain resort with his wife and children. He becomes ill and develops a high fever—104°. The cause seems to be unknown. The second day a doctor, a well-known specialist and family friend, arrives and visits him. He studies the symptoms and decides to begin a treatment after supper. His wife does all she can to make him comfortable, then hurriedly goes down to the dining room for a rapid meal.

The sick man feels very low. Suddenly he thinks of Padre Pio. " If you really have such power with God, you might show it now. Help me out of this! "

Instantly he is completely cured. He feels perfectly well. He has no fever. He gets up, dresses and begins to shave. He is standing near the open window. His wife enters, is terrified. She fears he is delirious—about to fall from the window. The doctor arrives. The fever is measured and re-measured. Amazed, the doctor has to admit that his patient is in every way normal and in perfect health.

The Onorevole has an appointment with his original guide and friend to return to Padre Pio very soon.

*Nerina's Cigarette.*

A number of years ago, my friend Nerina Noe, daughter of the former well-known Professor Noe of the faculty of the University of Santiago, Chile, who at present has a Montessori kindergarten in Rome, was quite impressed by my " cigarette story:, that is, the grace I had obtained of losing my desire for smoking from one moment to another. She is a very refined person of delicate tastes and when she went, shortly thereafter, to San Giovanni Rotondo and subsequently to confession to Padre Pio, and told him that she was thinking of giving up smoking, she did not expect the rather gruff reply she was given: " Le donne che fumano fanno schifo," (Women who smoke cigarettes are disgusting.) She emerged, feeling almost offended. However, she did notice that cigarettes attracted her less and, for a number of months, she did not smoke at all.

She was telling me this one night in Chiavari the following summer and she added, " . . . and you know a few weeks ago at a tea in the Chilean Embassy, I lit one just as a gesture, as one does on such occasions, but I had to put it out immediately. ' perché mi faceva schifo ' (because I found it disgusting.) Then she stopped short, never until that moment realizing that the same word used by Padre Pio—" schiffo "—had escaped from her lips, she too had been granted the grace given to me. A little play of words! How often Padre Pio attempts to produce a bit of confusion in order to hide the grace one is receiving at the time.


*Wanda.*


Wanda is from the province of Udine. She has on two occasions, spent months in a cast after operations on her hip. She has endured great suffering and has, through Padre Pio's prayers, already obtained a great grace: shortly after the removal of the cast, she was able to kneel and pray, flexibility having returned instantly. She feels she could not live through another

183

such ordeal, and yet the specialists are already pro-
jecting a third operation. She comes to Padre Pio to
thank him for the grace obtained, and in confession
tells him that the doctors wish to operate again. She is
desperate and Padre Pio consoles her, saying that he
does not agree with the doctors, that another operation
is not necessary. She goes home happily but the bone
specialists in Bologna insist that she must submit to
further surgery because xrays show that one fall would
irreparably shatter all previous work. Confused and
disheartened, despite Padre Pio's counsel, she goes to
Bologna and enters the hospital. In the days of prepar-
ation before surgery, she falls twice on the marble
floors of the hospital. Nothing happens! She remembers
Padre Pio's words, packs her suitcase and leaves.
Fifteen years have since passed. She leads a normal
life with no more hip trouble despite what x-rays
show.

## To Walk!

Another hip-bone case even more startling. This
woman whom we met at San Giovanni Rotondo tells
us that she was born with a congenital hip condition
and, from childhood, had always been obliged to use
two special canes in order to walk. When a fully-grown
woman, she comes to San Giovanni Rotondo. During
the night she dreams that two large hands appear, place

themselves on her hips and press them closely together. She has the sensation that the bones have somehow gone into place and, in fact, she awakens to find herself cured—her hips straightened and strong. She is able to walk and run in completely normal fashion. When we met her a number of years had already passed. She was successfully employed in Rome, and could out-walk us all.

*Man with a Satchel.*

September, 1967: My friend, Anna Baroni, a pharmacist from Chiavari, tells me this little story of a couple she met at the pensione at San Giovanni Rotondo. They are from Potenza in Calabria. They have three growing children. The wife tells Anna that her husband has been a spiritual son of Padre Pio for years—even prior to their marriage. At the time of their engagement, and during the early months of their marriage, this devotion of her husband to Padre Pio annoys her. Shortly after their marriage he brings her to San Giovanni Rotondo. She is not overly impressed, and the day she sees, upon entering their room, the frame that had contained their wedding picture, now bearing the photograph of Padre Pio, she loses her temper and, looking at the image, mutters words meaning (more or less): " You even had to stick your nose in here! "
They return home and, after some months, the time

arrives for the birth of their first child. Everything presents itself very badly—a normal birth seems impossible. As she lies there suffering intensely, she suddenly thinks in her desperation of Padre Pio. " Oh," she says almost resentfully, " If you really are our saintly protector, you might come and give me a hand now."

The symptoms change and the birth takes place with ease and normalcy. After, as she lies quietly resting, at the foot of her bed she suddenly sees Padre Pio! " You called me," he says a bit gruffly, " and so here I am." She is overcome with emotion and wishes she could throw herself at his feet, but, in less than a minute, he has disappeared.

The strange part of this vision however, is that it includes another man who stands behind Padre Pio. He is hatless and wears a raincoat. In his hand he grips the handle of a small, roundish satchel. She is able to see his face with absolute clearness and insists that she could identify him among a hundred other men. The memory of his face never leaves her. Some persons. trying to analyze the happening, have suggested to her that evidently due to the shape of the suitcase, he is a doctor, and since Padre Pio is in front of him it means that he has preceded the doctor, but, somehow, this explanation does not satisfy her since this man is not a shadowy symbol of a doctor but a very decided person—with a very decided face.

She becomes obsessed with the desire to find this person and on their next visit to Padre Pio, she scans all faces in her search for him, having a feeling that he is here at San Giovanni Rotondo.

One afternoon, as they are in church for rosary and benediction, her attempt to look intently at each man who comes into view annoys her husband who, in his soft, southern Italian accent says, " After all, it was only a dream! "

The next morning, he is among the number of men who are awaiting Padre Pio's arrival in the sacristy. When he enters and passes in their midst, he stops before her husband just long enough to say, almost reprovingly: " And so, it was only a dream eh? "

In time, I am certain we will find the missing key to the satchel!

*Voice from the Past.*

A woman enters Padre Pio's confessional for the first time. Padre Pio is heard to say in a stern, raised voice, " E non senti piangere nulla? " (" Don't you hear a crying voice? ") " No," replies the bewildered woman. " You don't hear the sound of crying? " thunders Padre Pio a second time. " No," again replies the more than confused woman. " ... That child you murdered years ago ... " The woman emerges in a flood of tears.

Later, she will explain that many years before she had been guilty of a wilfully provoked abortion. She thought it was buried in her past; she, herself, had almost forgotten. She had evidently confessed this sin long years ago but—and here is the point—she had been unwilling to realize the gravity of her act, and had never truly repented sufficiently. For this reason he pulled it out of her past—otherwise he would have let it remain quietly where it was, adverse as he is to a scrupulous returning to sins for which one has already sincerely repented. Surely the woman now knows a deeper and a lasting peace.

## A Question of Pace

I received as a gift, a little booklet from a Dublin friend entitled: « It is not necessary to burn in Purgatory." It is written by a Jesuit and has the Imprimatur of the church.

I cannot deny that the idea is rather pleasing to me. A few months later, at San Giovanni Rotondo, in my confession, among other sins and negligences, I add: " Padre, sometimes I am a bit lazy." " Oh," replies Padre Pio quick as a flash, " and you expect to go DIRECTLY to heaven at this pace? "

## Never Breakfast.

I am San Giovanni Rotondo with a chubby, well—nourished friend whom we will call Angelina. It is still the period when one must fast from midnight in order to receive Holy Communion, which Padre Pio distributes about nine-thirty every morning. She desires ardently to receive the Divine Host from his hands but hunger and the habit of an early and substantial breakfast always impede her. We discuss this problem daily. I try to explain that, perhaps if she changed the hour of her breakfast and diminished the quantity gradually, after a certain number of days she probably could arrive at the nine-thirty hour in a fasting condition, but to no avail.

Dawns her confession morning. After an exchange of words back and forth between her and Padre Pio, such as: " E tu vuoi andare in paradiso in carrozza? " (meaning, more or less, " And you want to get to heaven riding in a carriage? ") he asks her. " Do you say your morning prayers? " " I quite often forget," she replies.
" But never your breakfast, eh?! "

*A Healing Reprimand.*

A woman is weeping and protesting in a corner of the restaurant at San Giovanni Rotondo. She has been to confession to Padre Pio. She is surrounded by a group of consoling, well-meaning but not at the moment, very enlightened souls. She had a few months before suffered the loss of her twenty-year old daughter in child-birth. She cannot reconcile herself nor think of anything else. She has come to Padre Pio to be consoled. She expects sweet, soft words. She is shocked and shaken when, to her amazement, a decided and rather stern voice scolds her: " And why are you weeping so much for her when she is already in Paradise? You would do much better to devote more attention to the activities of your seventeen-year-old-daughter who comes home late at night from dances and entertainments! "

*Easter Eggs.*

I have hesitated about writing this little episode, wondering about its effect upon the reader. However, I have decided that if God let it happen it can be told. I know the reader will remember that I am writing honestly, and under God's gaze.

Very briefly, I will say that later in the year of Daisy's and my first visit to San Giovanni Rotondo, we returned to spend Easter in our little church with Padre Pio. We do not think of writing ahead to reserve a room and, upon arriving two days before Easter, we find all rooms in the little pensione occupied and all hotels crowded. We therefore have to content ourselves with a " left-over "—a wretched room where we spend two indescribable days sleeping almost dressed with our coats spread on top of the rusty old beds. Let us simply say it is a " Good Friday " room. On Easter we are to find better quarters but, for these two days, we do consume a bit of our purgatory.

Daisy now confesses to me that, during this stay she had often thought of the traditional custom of her native Florence of bringing hard-boiled eggs to church Easter morning to be blessed and of beginning Easter day with the consumption of these eggs. She thought of how much she would have liked to begin Easter with eggs blessed at Padre Pio's Mass, but in our dark, damp dungeon, we had sufficient complications without introducing eggs into the scene.

Imagine her surprise and amazement therefore, when upon emerging from the five o'clock Easter Mass, she finds two hard-boiled eggs in the pocket of her coat! And imagine our delight as we sit in the little bar eating our Easter eggs with a glass of vermouth, feeling like two children rewarded for their two days of penance, and certain that this is the happiest Easter we have ever spent.

This happening, like the " Rosary story " is interesting to me not so much for the event in itself, as for the fact that it was the fulfillment of a hidden wish, a personal desire, in neither case spoken of. A confirmation, therefore, that we are never alone—that we are always accompanied by an invisible force that reads our hearts and thoughts.

What greater consolation can man have?

*Skeptical Bishop.*

We are told that a bishop once declared to Pope Benedict XV., words to the effect that he had no faith in Padre Pio. " Padre Pio is a man of God," replies His Holiness, " go and see for yourself."

The bishop obeys the Pope's order and leaves incognito for San Giovanni Rotondo. Upon arriving at the station of Foggia, he is, much to his surprise, greeted by two monks who are awaiting him. Upon his marveling, he receives these words in answer: " Padre Pio tells us that your excellency has been sent by His Holiness, the Pope."

The bishop has enough; he understands. His opinion changed, and, going to the ticket window to buy a return ticket to Rome, he says to the amazed monks; " I have not the courage to face Padre Pio. With the ' information service ' he has at his disposal, I do not want to hear repeated the words I used in speaking of him to His Holiness."

*Styles and Fashions*

Padre Pio has rarely been so insistent on any subject as on that of the present-day lack of modesty in dress. He is so insistent, in fact, that any of us who

Padre Pio encounters an International group of visiting bishops

Photo Ariston

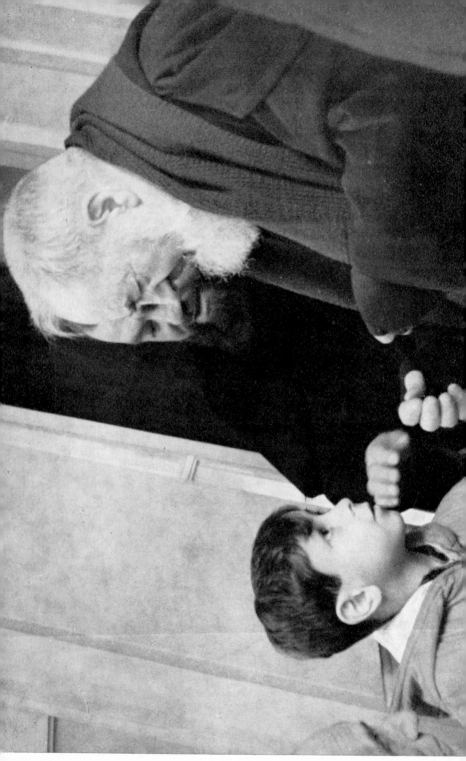

ounters a young friend

Abresch

encounters a tragic problem

Photo Michele

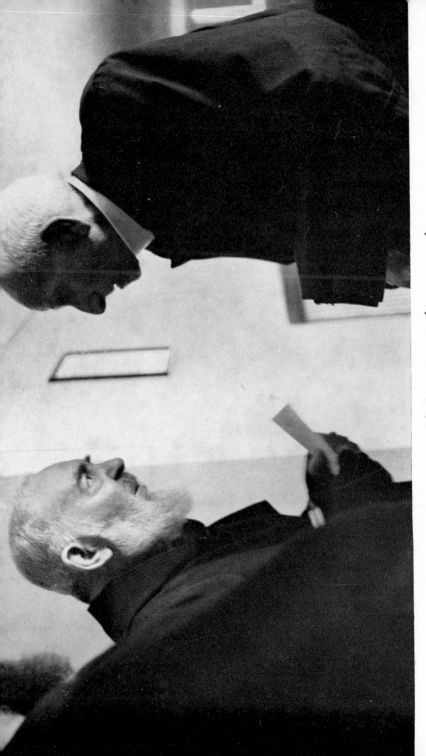

*encounters an elderly priest seeking counsel*

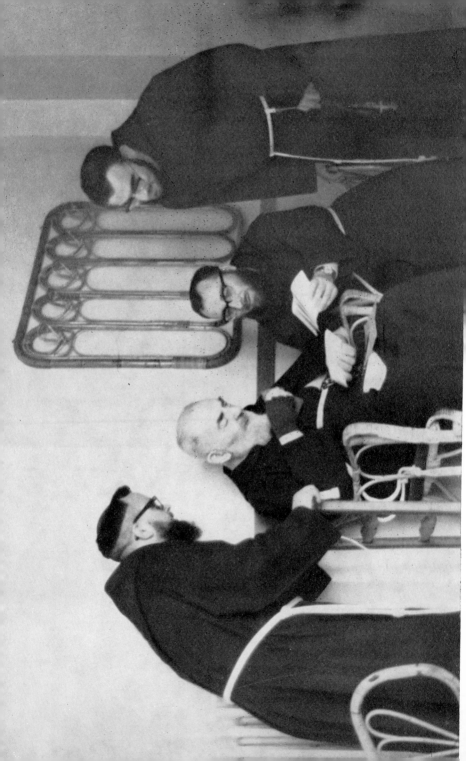

approach his confessional wearing a skirt that is not below the knee is sent flying unconfessed. (I have been included in this group!)

He feels that depsite the coming and going of fashions we should keep within a proper limit—on the right—and, conservative side, not on the left-and, provocative side of fashions for as he says, " We cannot have two Masters."

In this moment I am thinking of the confidences made to me by various young men, university students (one getting a third degree from the University of California) on this subject. Their thoughts and observations might be surprising to a great many modern day young women. These intelligent, attractive young men feel the need of breathing a bit of clean spiritual air near Padre Pio.

But suffice it to say that Padre Pio has entreated us all to make a point of speaking of this subject, doing all we can to meliorate this condition. It may be an unpopular topic, and yet if he who reads in so many souls, and understands the origin and causes of sinful depravation and tragedy, sees fit to place such emphasis on this problem, it must have much deeper roots than we, superficially see. Perhaps the way we, and others are dressed has a much more profound influence on us—our way of thinking, and therefore, acting—than we know.

To that talented group known as the designers of fashion who have been given a very special gift and responsibility by God, let me say that Padre Pio has promised that a very special blessing will follow those who work toward bettering this condition. Those, who in working hard to design beautiful clothes, will remember to add just a little more of—shall we say—" dignity."

When Padre Pio says a " SPECIAL BLESSING," he means a " SPECIAL BLESSING! "

Part V

# *ILLUMINATION*

# Paolo from Paris

It is the summer of 1966 at San Giovanni Rotondo. Our little pensione has grown much larger. Rooms have been added, meals are now served. There is a constant flow of new and old clientele.

Among the new is Paolo. He is totally blind and has come alone all the way from Paris. He has not come in regard to his physical eyes—that is, to ask for the return of his eyesight for the simple reason that he has had no eyes since the age of ten when a kettle of boiling water completely destroyed them.

He is a nice looking man of about thirty-five, above average in intelligence, with a college degree from the Sorbonne. He teaches in a girls' Catholic high school and has published a book or two dealing with philosophical subjects if I remember correctly. He is a bit proud, or perhaps I should say reserved, not wont to reveal what is enclosed in his heart but the black mourning band on his lapel jacket speaks for itself. It is worn for the loss of his mother a few months before. He has no brothers or sisters, and his father, a military man, died when he was but four years old.

Under such circumstances, one can easily imagine the ties there were between mother and son, and what a void her death must have left in Paolo's everyday life.

He is, intellectually and religiously speaking, a serious-minded young man. Fortunately he speaks Italian as well as English, and so will be able to go to confession to Padre Pio.

Due to the fact that it is summer, the height of the season at San Giovanni Rotondo, the pensione is filled to overflowing and for this reason, and also because of his missing eyesight, he is given one of the worst rooms in the house, next to the hot, noisy kitchen, but which, in compensation, is located close to the garden entrance, close to the dining room—avoiding staircases and other complications for him. Because of these disagreeable factors concerning his room and the heat of the August night, I suggest a little walk, a breath of air. He readily accepts. I take him up to the rustic pasture land under Padre Pio's cell window where people habitually go to receive his good-night, and his midday benediction. We turn our backs to the purple hills sharply outlined against the luminous sky, and to the white convent in its wall-encircled garden of shadowy, ancient cypress trees, to face the wide open spaces below where the gulf of Manfredonia in the distance shimmers in the moonlight. Paolo is enraptured by the description of the scene—he seems to " see " everything, and even interrupts to add, " oh, yes . . . and all around the curve of the gulf are the little lights of the town of Manfredonia. How beautiful. How beautiful." (The town and its lights had not been spoken of.) With some strange inner eye he is able to visualize everything—

to drink it in together with the soft summer air, and the mysterious immensity and peace.

Sauntering back, we speak of Padre Pio, of the pensione, of the hours, local atmosphere, customs of the place in general. Before leaving him in his room, he has to be shown where the bathroom is—each faucet and gadget—the door to avoid that opens on a staircase to the floor below.

In the kitchen, the clatter is still going on. His room is empty as the man with whom he is sharing it has not yet reentered. Paolo does not even know where his suitcases are. We discover them in a corner and manage to hoist them up onto the table.

After extracting his shaving kit and portable typewriter and some clean clothing, and discovering his bed, he seems happier, for he is at the point of exhaustion after his long hot trip—more than twenty-four hours of sitting up on the train from Paris. I bid him goodnight, promising to take him down the road to buy postcards in the morning.

These details have been written purposely so that the reader can grasp what heroic courage it took for him to face such a long, complicated trip alone. For it is not the big moves of a journey such as this that represent the main problems or the greatest nervous tensions. Some kind person or other, seeing the dark glasses plus the blind man's white cane, will always assist the traveler in crossing streets, changing trains, and will guide him about the railroad station. But once arrived, a small pensione can represent a great torment and anguish, a new world which one must explore, discover in darkness, totally dependent upon others. Such a confusion of people and voices and strange situations all at once! For a sensitive person such as Paolo, the first few days are truly an ordeal.

The following morning, I accompanied him to the nearby book and postal shop, in order to select cards for him to mail to Paris. They are for nuns at the school where he teaches, and are, according to their wishes, photographs of Padre Pio. From my descriptions he chooses a postal of Padre Pio with the Divine Host in his hand, the selection of which prophetic card will later make us smile.

On our return walk the conversation is of Padre Pio. I attempt to answer his many questions, describing his personality, his few words, his limited time, but also his thorough understanding of each person with whom he comes in contact, and of his true needs. I advise him to make his confession as simple and concise as possible and after receiving absolution to ask, with clearness and brevity, the counsel or grace which he has come so far to obtain.

The days pass interminably for Paolo! His roommate, Pietro, takes an interest in him, escorts him up to receive Padre Pio's blessing when he passes to greet the men visitors in the morning, and also sees to it that he is comfortably seated on the low garden wall under the almond trees, with his typewriter, before going off about his own affairs.

At meals, too, (one of his worst problems,) after being bounced about from table to table by the unthinking little maid, he is finally placed with a young magistrate from Rome and his eleven year old son. He is assisted with great delicacy and the conversation is easy, natural, brilliant.

Things have improved since those first, extremely trying days but each one is still a bit of a martyrdom, and he is tensely waiting for *that* confession, for *that* counsel.

Finally dawns the day! We are all hoping he will find in that confessional all that he needs and has travelled so far to obtain. But to our chagrin Paolo emerges with a drawn, pallid face, and frozenly expressive words: " Padre Pio should not have treated me this way! Padre Pio should not have treated me this way! "

By degrees he tells us how things went. He began his confession naturally by saying that he had gone to confession fifteen days before in Paris, proceeding with his usual, normal confession, assuring us that it contained no especially grave or serious sin. At its termination, instead of words of spiritual advice or absolution, our poor astonished Paolo hears a very decided Padre Pio say in a very decided voice: " Quindici giorni di buio. No! Non ti dò l'assoluzione! " Fifteen days of darkness. No! I will not give you absolution! " And, with these words without giving Paolo time to utter a syllable, the confession comes to an abrupt and dramatic end, leaving Paolo in a shell-shocked state of mind, rebellious and hurt, deeply so. When, with his room-mate Pietro, he had encountered Padre Pio as he passed among the men visitors, he had called him paternally and affectionately by name, he had placed his hand upon his head—had shown every sign of observing and understanding him . . . and now, after such a long, penance-filled, expensive trip, and the need he felt for assistance in his mysterious problem, an ending such as this was truly an unexpected blow—almost an unbearable and seemingly unpardonable one. All we can keep repeating is that Padre Pio has a technique of his own, that he very often withholds absolution when he wants strongly to drive a point home. Therefore it has not been denied for the usual reason. It is certain that it is only a temporary withholding in order to make him meditate , to search for the cause; to find a decided illumination of some sort. It is a method used by Padre Pio perhaps more frequently with those come from afar who may never accost him again—therefore a " strong dose," all at once, in a case of special need. We all try to put our finger on the vital point of this mystery. Paolo is becoming rigid and is very evidently going to pass a bad and sleepless night, but all in vain—the key is still missing. Reluctantly we bid him goodnight and sadly go to bed.

Upon awakening in the morning, a new clearness: the key is certainly contained in the words " . . . fifteen days of darkness." Therefore, definitely in the period from his last confession to now.

At the breakfast hour there is Paolo as expected —tired, haggard and grim. " Paolo," I think I have found the answer; tell me, have you received Holy Communion in this period—in the fifteen days since your last confession in Paris? " " No," says Paolo, " not once." " Well, Paolo, there is your answer. You naturally did not mention this fact but Padre Pio saw that you were without the Divine Presence of Our Lord, the True Illuminator. This is what he wants you to understand, very emphatically, for the future."

Paolo's intelligent face changes expression. He understands immediately; the explanation satisfies him—makes sense. He begins to change color—is smilingly relieved.

He decides that Pietro will take him up to the convent and have Padre Pio asked if the interpretation of his confessional words is as we have concluded.

Later, at lunch, we will find a radiant Paolo—everything is clear and as we thought, absolution granted. Paolo had been given the first place in the file of men who await Padre Pio's passage at the noon hour. Padre Pio, upon arriving, had deliberately stopped before Paolo, paternally placing his hand upon his head, making him feel his presence by strongly pressing his half-gloved stigmatized hand against Paolo's cheek. " Padre," says Paolo, " prega che io abbia la Luce." (" Padre, pray that I be given light.") " Ma si," (" But yes,") Padre Pio answers with great emphasis and tenderness.

Paolo understands that he and his problem have been thoroughly understood—that Padre Pio is near him spiritually— that he has entered in his great current of prayer, and, most of all, he has learned where to look to fill the void he perhaps feels inside of himself. The " Great Friend " who will never falter or fail him, upon whose love he will always be able to count and by whom he will feel truly embraced and guided.

Will he perhaps marry? I do not know, but he has become aware that he must not lean too much on human affection only—that everything must come secondary to the Other, and that the great " Enlightener " whom he will now carry in his daily life and heart will assist him always in all his needs, in what he is humanly groping to find. And, above all, He will help him to find himself—his true self, and therefore his true road.

The next morning, five of us drive to the grotto of St. Michael, thrity-five miles distant. We describe to Paolo the rather desolate countryside with its gray, rocky formations emerging from the overall green and its tiny stone shepherds' huts scattered all along the way. Also the ruins of an old monastery where hundreds of years ago, especially prior to the 13th century, the pilgrims who trod these parts on their long journeys to the grotto found hospitality and rest. We have been told that this territory is very similar to that of the Holy Land, and as we go higher and higher, curving tortuously around the mountainside to climb the 400 meters that elevate Monte Sant'Angelo from San Giovanni Rotondo, the already small shepherd huts become miniature and the whole panorama seems part of a Christmas Nativity scene. One can easily imagine the angels singing to the shepherds on Christmas Eve—as they did almost two thousand years ago in Bethlehem—dispersed on hills such as these.

We tell Paolo that among the long list of saints, emperors, and other well-known personages that had come great distances by land and sea, suffering enormous difficulties and hardships of such an undertaking in order to visit this famous sanctuary,is St. Francis of Assisi, who upon arriving at the entrance of the grotto, felt the angelic air so strongly that he, humbly, deeming himself unworthy to enter, did not proceed any further, contenting himself to kneel in prayer at the threshold where a poor, blind young girl sat begging for alms.

Before leaving, we are told that he blessed her, whereupon she regained her sight.

For this reason, immediately on entering, on the righthand side of the two great bronze and silver doors which give access to the sanctuary, is to be found an altar dedicated to St. Francis with a painting representing the scene of this miracle.

Finally, our taxi takes the last curve of our ascent and the sanctuary suddenly bursts into view together with, high on the right, the famous ruins of a Norman castle inhabited in different eras by various kings and princes.

As we descend the long, time worn, rocky steps that lead down to the grotto, the sensation always returns of leaving time behind us; of living, for a moment at least, where all things are ONE.

Stars, planets, spaces and universes become small, insignificant. Only one thing seems enormous—the infinite mystery of the ALTOGETHER of these things. We pass through the two great doors (ecumenical doors, I should say,) upon which are depicted scenes from the old and new testaments with the angels manifesting themselves in both, forming a liason between the two, one door representing the old, the other the new, but when closed, forming but one entity.

We go to the altar rail and recite, together with Paolo, the act of consecretion to St. Michael, remaining in silent prayer. After a complete tour and description of the grotto, with its high artistic and archeological interest, we, by degrees, rewind our steps upwards, pausing only to throw a glance of farewell at the two gothic doors that form the entrance to the stone steps from which we have just emerged. We have spent more time below than anticipated. Our taxi driver is silent and grim. We climb in as rapidly as possible and begin our return trip. It is a splendid summer morning and a mysterious inner happiness pervades all of us. The sun-splashed valley below with its toy houses seems to have lost its desolate aspect and returns our smiling gaze. Pietro and Paolo are both tranquil—extremely serene— and now, softly, someone intones the " Ave Maria " sung at Lourdes. All join, and the voices are truly stupendous, perfectly blended in pitch and tone. Even our stern-faced driver begins to move his head back and forth; he is carried away and begins to sing with us in a splendid tenor voice. I look below and think again of that first Christmas Eve . . . of the shepherds and the angelic choir: " Peace on earth to men of good will. "

Paolo is smiling, thinking of many things, perhaps of the " key " to the great new peace he has found. Tomorrow when we will place him on the bus that will take him below to his Paris-bound train, in the care of friends, we will hear his deeply sincere words, " I will never forget Padre Pio and San Giovanni Rotondo! " spoken with a joy and gratitude that will later send us all into church with a softly murmured " Thank you! "

Dear Paolo, if you should ever read these pages, I hope you will feel a great satisfaction in knowing that you, who do not see physically, have been used as an instrument of God to help others see spiritually. It will be you who will take them under your wing and help them cross their confused roads and troubled paths.

For the faith that brought you alone to San Giovanni Rotondo, your penance, your sleepless nights in that miserable room, have borne perhaps much greater fruit than you thought, not only for you but for others. The message Padre Pio so emphatically wanted you to receive from those confessional words is not only meant for you but for all of us, and particularly the many Catholics who struggle along in, at best, a semi-darkness when they could have the Divine Host in their hearts— the Great Friend, flooding them with His light, and His love, and His supernatural strength, to help them bear the crosses inevitably encountered by us all in our earthly journey.

> " I am the living bread which came down from heaven. If any man eat of this bread, he shall live forever; and the bread that I will give is my flesh, for the life of the world."
>
> (John: 51-52) Douay.

*Padre Pio distributing Holy Comunion.*     Photo Abresch

## Padre Pio says...

" The most beautiful " Credo " is that which bursts from your lips in moments of darkness, sacrifice and pain, in the supreme effort of an inflexible will toward that which is good. Like a lightening flash it rips open the darkness of your soul, lifts you from the tempest, and leads you to God."

" . . . it is in meditation and prayer that we find God."

" Walk with simplicity in the way of the Lord; do not torment your spirit."

" Let us very often pause, and praying, place our trust in Divine Providence. We may be certain that heaven and earth shall pass away sooner than Our Lord will fail to protect us."

" My past, Oh Lord, to your Mercy;
My present, Oh Lord, to your Love;
My future, Oh Lord, to your Providence."

" The field of battle between God and Satan is the human soul. It is in the soul that it rages every moment of our life. The soul must give free access to the Lord so that it can be fortified by Him. It must be clothed with Jesus Christ, with His justice and truth, with the shield of faith and the word of God, in order to conquer such a powerful enemy. To be clothed with Jesus Christ it is necessary to die to oneself."

" . . . Sometimes as I pray Our Divine Lord presents to me souls never met or known saying, ' Pray for these.' "

## A LETTER FROM PADRE PIO

From " L'Osservatore Romano," official Vatican newspaper, I quote (translating) parts of a letter written by Padre Pio to His Holiness, Pope Paul VI., only a few weeks before his death. The occasion was a special audience granted to the Fathers " Capitolari " of the Franciscan Order by Pope Paul:

Your Holiness.

I take advantage of this encounter to unite myself spiritually to my brothers, to place humbly at your feet, my affectionate greeting, and personal devotion; my love, faith, and obedience to the dignity of Him whom you represent upon this earth.

The Capuchin order has always been in the first row in its loving devotion, fidelity and obedience to the Holy See. My prayer to God is that such it shall remain, continuing always in its profound religious austerity, and evangelical poverty, and that yet, while observing faithfully these rules that form its constitution it may renew itself in vitality and interior spirituality as indicaed by Vatican Council II., in order to be always more adequately prepared to go to the assistance of the many necessities of Mother Church, as directed by Your Holiness.

I well understand what profound afflictions you carry in your heart in these days for the lot of the Church, for world peace, for the many necessities of the people; but, above all for the lack of spirit of obedience of a certain number of Catholics as to the enlightened teachings that you, assisted by the Holy Spirit, and in the name of God, have given us.

Permit me, as your humble spiritual son, to offer you my daily prayer and suffering, imploring God to comfort you with His grace in order that you may continue ahead, in your straight and arduous path, in the defence of those eternal truths that remain unaltered with the changing times.

I thank you also, in the name of my spiritual children and " Prayer groups " for the clear and decided words you have given us, particularly in the last encyclical, " Humanae Vitae," and I reaffirm my faith, my unconditional obedience to your illuminated instructions.

May Our Lord concede the triumph of the truth, peace to His church, tranquility to all the people of the earth, health and prosperity to Your Holiness, in order that with the passing of these clouds the Kingdom of God may triumph in all hearts through your apostolic work as Supreme Pastor of all Christianity.

I kneel before you, asking your blessing, united with my franciscan brothers, as well as with my spiritual children, prayer groups, and my sick and suffering, for all the charitable efforts, that in the name of Jesus, and under your protection, we endeavor to bring into being.

The submissive son of Your Holiness

(signed) P. Pio - Cappuccino

September 12, 1968
San Giovanni Rotondo

Part VI

# *CONCLUSION*

# Regina Pacis: A Message for All

It is eleven o'clock at night—late October. The Rome train is nearing Chiavari.

I am feeling tired physically and let down emotionally. After a week spent together in Rome, my brother and sister-in-law have taken the plane for Chicago. I feel quite alone. Through Padre Pio's prayers and advice they had arrived in time to drink a last happy glass of champagne with Mother, console and brighten her last hours, and share and divide with me the moment of her departure from this world. Everything has worked out with Divine help.

All the pieces have gone together into place, one by one. Mother's suffering had not been too heavy, her morale high; we had been able to distract her—to keep her happy—and yet spiritually she was perfectly prepared, asking for the sacraments quite often. The boat is in port, so to speak, after long months of hiding the heaviness in my heart at the realization of what I knew— but she did not. After the social obligations of the funeral—of being serene hostess to all the callers— now, finally, the moment when all tension is lessened. Nothing more is required of one. All at once the weight of heartfelt sadness makes itself known—a terrible heaviness. I am met at the train by my cousins; my dear aunt opens the apartment door; I manage to say a few words of greeting and I proceed down the hall toward my room. Then the unexpected blow. The sitting-room that divides my room from Mother's! The room where we listened to our Beethoven concerts together, where we played Canasta in the evening . . . her brilliant red armchair, lighted directly by the white wedgewood lamp, empty, empty. The chair where I always found her sitting, waiting for me at the end of my journeys, full of chatter and gaiety. " Did you have a good time in Rome? How is Daisy? Did you have dinner at Gino's? Did you see the Pope? "

Emptiness and silence—always it is going to be—emptiness and silence.

My heart swells to unbearable proportions. No sign of tears, nothing but the horrible sensation that it is impossible to sustain what is happening inside of me, something with which I cannot cope—beyond my power. I am terrified at myself.

In my room in my anguished state, prayer seems impossible. An S.O.S. to the " Forces " above is the only despairing, terror-stricken type of prayer that emerges from me. I am sinking in stormy waters . . . . I cannot drag out more than a few words—repeating and repeating them, and here is the mystery—why I pick the words that I do . . . . " REGINA PACIS, ORA PRO NOBIS, REGINA PACIS, ORA PRO NOBIS . . . . over and over again I say this prayer and all at once, stretched out on my bed, wondering if I am going to die, something wonderful happens, something inexplicable. I do not see or hear anything but my room becomes flooded, permeated, with an immense sweetness and serenity. Something has passed; I do not exactly know what, but in one minute my anguish transforms itself into a joyous peace, peace and serenity—the security a small child experiences when held tightly in a mother's arms—I am being held warmly in spiritual arms. Extinguishing the light in my little lamp, in two minutes I am asleep, contentedly and blissfully asleep.

Perhaps there will be thoughts about this story, but only those who have passed through a similar anguish will know that, humanly speaking, such a complete transformation, in one minute, is impossible in the natural order. Personally, I know most definitely that it is, because I know how I felt.

Nevertheless, it is doubtful that I would have had the simplicity of recounting this very personal experience had it not been for one factor that will not let me rest—the particular words of this prayer, " Our Lady, Queen of Peace, pray for us. "

In the morning upon awakening from my refreshing sleep, a dawning conviction takes possession of me, a certainty that this grace has also been granted to me for a higher purpose—that of spreading this prayer—that God wants this prayer to be said—and so I begin telling members of our prayer group, here and there, to say " Regina Pacis, Ora Pro Nobis. " This is in the year 1961.

But now, in this unrestful 1968, I feel that perhaps God wants this message of prayer to be spread over a much wider range than our little prayer group. What happened to me, in a small way, can happen in a large way if many voices, sincerely imploring, raise this prayer daily toward heaven. There is absolutely no reason to believe that God loves me more than another creature, or that my prayer should obtain results denied to another. The force of this prayer has demonstrated itself in my life, why not in the lives of others? All the souls who are anguished or who are against war—mothers who have sons in the armed forces, can say this prayer. Why not open the road for God to act?

If this prayer is pleasing to Him and a spirit of peace can flood this hating world, it will be a clear demonstration that He wishes us to invoke His mother, Mary. An indication that now that Christians have learned to say the " Our Father " together, the time is also ripe to pray to His mother together. HE DOES NOT WANT HER TO BE A SYMBOL OF DIVISION AMONG CHRISTIANS, BUT ONE OF UNITY. And, bluntly speaking, if she is good enough for Him, certainly she should be good enough for us. If He called her " Mother," what joy and privilege for us to be able to invoke her with the same name. How many political conferences for peace, for unity, for brotherly love, between countries and races—and yet all the world continues in turmoil. It seems so very evident that this universe can never achieve peace on a horizontal basis alone. The pieces will never fit. Until we have learned to search for it vertically, there is practically no hope of success of any serious dimension.

" Vertically " means spiritually, through the Gospels and prayer—a great deal of prayer because this great universal love, and therefore tolerance, can only descend from above us, from that great God of love who alone, by degrees, can fill us with His spirit. " WITHOUT ME YOU CAN DO NOTHING." And, if He has seen fit to fill His Mother's hands with blessings and graces beyond measure—blessings and peace—and desires us to invoke her intercession—wants her to be the dispenser—to be the one to help shower His love upon this needy world, to be the one to calm the storming sea—why should we small creatures object. He alone contains *all wisdom*. He listened to, and granted her wish at the wedding at Cana, changing the water into wine. She, part of our Divine Providence, anticipating events even before their moment of maturation.

Such a simple little prayer, and yet so potent when mixed with sincere good will! And, if said singly, and particularly in GROUPS—family, and household groups with children, before going to bed—and most important of all, Protestants and Catholics united—people of all races—I am very certain of the results. Christ will not deny to others what He granted, through His mother, to me. Padre Pio has promised God would bear witness. Oh, do begin forming these groups!

So many adventures man searches, and the greatest one of all—PRAYER—is often left untouched!

Let us close with Padre Pio's words regarding Mary:

" ONLY SHE IS ABLE TO CAPTURE AND CONTAIN ALL THE TORRENTS OF LOVE THAT POUR FORTH FROM THE HEART OF GOD. ONLY SHE IS WORTHY TO CORRESPOND TO THEM."

" ALL THINGS REFER THEMSELVES TO HER. EACH GRACE PASSES THROUGH HER HANDS."

# Salve Regina

Hail holy Queen Mother of mercy,

Our life, our sweetness, and our hope.

To thee do we cry, poor banished children of Eve,

To Thee do we send up our sighs,

Mourning and weeping in this valley of tears.

Turn then, most gracious Advocate.

Thine eyes of mercy towards us

And after this, our exile, show unto us

The blessed fruit of thy womb, Jesus

O, clement, O, loving, O, sweet Virgin Mary,

Pray for us, O, holy mother of God,

That we may be made worthy

Of the promises of Christ.

Amen.

*Padre Pio ... 81 years of age ... 50 years of stigmatization spent in prayer FOR OTHERS.*

Photo Michele

Part VII

# PADRE PIO'S DEATH

### A NOT PREMEDITATED
### ADDITION
### TO THIS BOOK

# Father Don Giovanni Rossi Speaks*

" When on the morning of the twenty-third of September the radio communicated the news of the passing of Padre Pio, a profound impact was felt in all parts of the world, both among Catholics and those of other beliefs.

Padre Pio had been neither an orator nor a writer, artist, or organizer; only a simple Franciscan monk. And yet from the year 1918, after which he remained closed in his little out-of-the-world convent at San Giovanni Rotondo, more and more numerous had become the crowds of people who, from all countries and from every cultural and social condition, illustrious and unknown, had flocked to him, to see him, to receive a personal word, to find in his confessional, with the pardon of their sins, his peace and faith.

I have known and venerated him for many years and in my last recent visit to him, our conversation

---

* Father Don Giovanni Rossi is one of the outstanding Christian figures of Italy today. He is the founder of the well known " Pro Civitate Christiana " of Assisi and Director of the highly regarded bi-monthly magazine " La Rocca."

was affectionate, and despite his great physical weakness, his eyes were limpid with supernatural beauty. He seemed a man filled with the Holy Spirit.

With the same extraordinary intuition that enabled him to see Our Divine Lord in the Holy Eucharist, he was able to read deeply into the human soul. And even though at times his answers were hard and brusque, his words always awakened resolutions of conversion and betterment, engulfing all in the immensity and joy of divine grace.

The Holy Mass and the Rosary were the great central moments of his whole day. He prayed and suffered constantly. Many say they have noticed a most fragrant perfume emerge from his person. This was not my lot. But if it is true that from the person of Jesus flowed a miraculous spiritual force, how can one doubt that from Padre Pio there should not flow a similar one, when he, stigmatized, could truthfully repeat with St. Paul: " It is now no longer I that live, but Christ that lives in me. (Gal. 2: 20).

I have heard of the miracles and bilocations of Padre Pio. All things are possible to God, and to the men who are His instruments and through whom He operates. Only the church will, in due time, give her secure judgment regarding these facts . . . .

But in me, personally, strongly rests the desire to remember that it is not so much his hospital, The

Home for the Relief of Suffering, which will remain in perpetual memory of Padre Pio, but that his name and person will last forever in time to tell us (and particularly us of the clergy) that above all that is movement, organization, and activity for apostolic work, SANCTITY is still the greatest force with which to testify, and to announce Jesus Christ to the world.

In the poverty and simplicity, humility and love of Padre Pio I perceive again the Resurrected Christ who, seen on the hills and lake of Galilee, has reappeared in this, our time ,as did St. Francis of Assisi in the thirteenth century."

# A Last Blessing

On September 22nd, 1968, I had the grace of finding myself at San Giovanni Rotondo, and of receiving that evening, Padre Pio's last earthly blessing.

At six o'clock he was still in church, bent in prayer. At two-thirty the following morning he quietly expired after clearly giving his last spiritual instructions and messages for all.

Some days later, after the funeral, as I sat in quiet meditation in the ancient little sanctuary of Santa Maria delle Grazia, the modest setting of so many spectacular happenings, two thoughts, two phrases, kept repeating and repeating themselves with ever-increasing conviction in my mind. With the subsiding of the confusion and emotion of the event, and the funeral (attended by over one hundred thousand persons from every country and every walk of life) these phrases emergd as though chiseled in the silence: " HE GAVE ALL! " and " ALL IS OF DIVINE DESIGN."

" HE GAVE ALL "—his last drop of blood, his last bit of breath. More than dying, he seemed completely consumed in his earthly mission. Of his bodily strength there had been practically nothing left and yet he died, as we say, with his boots on—active, heroically and yet serenely forcing himself to the last minute. For weeks no more blood had flowed from the stigmata, only a watery serum-like liquid—all that was left to give!

" ALL IS OF DIVINE DESIGN .... " How very many things inaugurated or concluded on this one single day—Sunday, September 22nd, 1968, that was destined to be Padre Pio's last!

Let us begin with the most important—the celebration that is, of Padre Pio's fifty years of stigmatization, for all the other events were correlated, or tied, to this fiftieth anniversary.

1) First of all, in honor of the occasion, representatives of his international prayer groups had been convened, from far and wide, to be present on this particular Sunday, so that, not only had they the joy and privilege of being with him on this occasion and of receiving his last blessing, but it was also destined that at the moment of his passing and for the following days, as for his funeral, Padre Pio had about him many of his most devoted spiritual children, as both he and they would have desired.

2) His Holiness, Pope Paul, had not only sent his affectionate message to honor the occasion, but also his official acknowledgment and approbation of these prayer groups so close to Padre Pio's heart.

3) On this day also, the first stone had been laid for the beautiful monumental bronze " Via Crucis " architecturally designed among the green pines of the sloping hillside adjacent to the hospital, the work of the famous sculptor Messina, Padre Pio's devoted spiri-

tual son who had wanted to dedicate his last great creation to him.

4) Also, and almost ironically, the crypt below the new church that his poor fellow monks had prepared as Padre Pio's place of burial, was finished and blessed by the bishop on that day. Certainly no one dreamed of such an immediate occupancy!

5) On Saturday, September 21, Padre Pio had suffered a very weak spell and had not been able to appear for his usual five o'clock Mass, but on Sunday he had not disappointed the bulging crowds that had come from every direction to be present on this day, and descending at five o'clock, he had not only found the strength and breath to say his usual Mass, but actually to sing it! A true swan song!

At the end, he had to be assisted, half fainting, to leave the altar, but in the evening toward six he reappeared in Church for Benediction, at the termination of which he gave all a last blessing.

At one o'clock the following morning he quietly called Padre Pellegrino, the young monk who slept in a cell adjacent in order to assist him in all his needs. Padre Pio had tears in his eyes and expressed the desire to arise. This was not unusual ,as he often arose at this hour in order to pray, recite the Holy Rosary and prepare himself for his five o'clock Mass.

Upon arising, instead of being assisted in his movements as was usual, he walked alone with great lightness to his little enclosed terrace and sat down in his wicker armchair. " Pellegrino," he said to his young assistant— " have you said your Mass yet? "—" But no," replied

Padre Pellegrino, astounded, " it is so early Padre . . . "
" Well, then, tomorrow you will say it for me." A
pause and then, " Pellegrino, in case God should call
me tonight, I would like to ask the pardon of all for
the trouble I have caused—assistance I have needed."
" But Padre . . . " " Pellegrino, in case God should call
me tonight, I should like to thank everyone and ask
all to pray for my soul."

Padre Pellegrino began to notice the increasing pallor,
the cold perspiration on Padre Pio's brow. He wanted
to call for assistance but was stopped. " Do not disturb
anyone, I would like you to confess me."

At the termination, the pallor, now unearthly, alarmed
Padre Pellegrino . . . but he was again detained by
Padre Pio's, " Do not disturb anyone."

A last series of messages and instructions—among
which a particular blessing for all his spiritual children,
his sick, his prayer groups and then, despite the agony
he was now enduring with his typical heroism, humility,
and consideration, he added, " It is best that this blessing be imparted by the Padre Guardiano (" Father
Superior.") Padre Pellegrino, now refusing to be detained, rushed for assistance. The doctor arrived, injections,
oxygen, . . . the monks arrived . . . the holy oils . . .
the Last Sacrament—Extreme Unction . . . But Padre
Pio, with closed eyes continued repeatedly to murmur
but two words " Gesu . . . Maria . . . " " Gesu . . .
Maria . . . " " Jesus . . . Mary . . . Jesus . . . . " Mary
At two-thirty those ardently loved names slipped from
his lips for the last time.

And so in twenty-four hours how many things
combined on that fiftieth anniversary. The fifty years

of suffering—of holocaust God had asked of Padre Pio in answer to his offer (for us!)

With what artistry all had been designed . . . the hand of the King of Artists. And with what artistry we, by staying close to Padre Pio, had been slipped more and more, immersed and lost, in the mysterious immensity that is the love of God!

As Doctor Valdoni, internationally famous professor of surgery at the University of Rome, one of Padre Pio's most devoted spiritual sons, said at the funeral: " One must surrender before the imponderable. "

And now that a good number of weeks have passed since his death, the first sense of loss has begun to fade away. His spiritual nearness is felt, more perhaps, than before, now that he is in God—and how gloriously powerful his intercession for us!

The Road is more than ever open for, since his death the constant flow of graces and miracles have continued to be reported just as when he was still alive, and he, seen in bilocation as before his passing. An example is the case reported authentically in Padre Pio's monthly periodical, " Home for the Relief of Suffering. "

Antonio Badolino, a resident of Foggia, aged fifty-three, for thirty-three years unable to sit or walk as a result of a terrible accident; medical history reads as follows: " Ankiliotic arthritis of the left hip resulting from fracture of the pelvis, the neck of the right femur and fracture of the left hip in a subject with a serious deficiency of the cardio-respiratory function ensuing from pulmonary factors, and with chronic generalized polyarthritis. " He had already been interned fifty four times in hospitals all over Italy, visited and operated

230

upon numerous times by the best bone surgeons with very little success, when he was brought by ambulance to Padre Pio's hospital, urgently in need of oxygen. A few nights after his arrival, he was visited by a monk who commanded him to get up and walk. Despite his insistence that he could not, some mysterious force impelled him to obey. Struggling and perspiring, he accompanied his strange director in silently visiting the bedside of each patient in the rooms of his corridor. Upon their return, he heard the following words as a leave-taking: " Don't forget to go down to the church to visit my tomb." Only then did he realize that it was Padre Pio whom he had never seen and in whom he had never believed. (In fact, he was an atheist who, because of his exasperated state, specialized in swearing at, and cursing all who came near.) The following day he was dancing and jumping about with no one's assistance for the first time in thirty-three years, with no shortness of breath or increase in pulse rate. The real miracle, however, is his total conversion and docility, and his constant visits of fervent prayer to the chapel.

My own consolation, however, rests in the fact that I once asked Padre Pio at the conclusion of a confession: " Padre, will you help me? " His reply came in one word which at this moment reaches down to me from heaven. " *Always* "—a prophetic word forming the bridge which unites our two worlds, not only for me but for all who beg his intercession in imploring from Our Lord and the Blessed Virgin the graces ardently desired.

It would appear that we can with certainty repeat the words of Enrico Medi, Professor of Terrestrial Physics at the University of Rome, and former Vice-President of Euratom in Brussels, one of Padre Pio's most humbly devoted sons who came to pray and comment for three hours on radio and television during Padre Pio's funeral: " We do not say ' we pray to God for you,' but rather, ' It is you who must continue to pray to God for us.' "

In concluding, I am certain Padre Pio would want us to return to the original ending of this book—an exhortation for the formation of prayer groups with intense prayer to Mary, Mother of God and Queen of Peace!

Padre Pio's dying prayer, a confirmation: " Gesú . . . Maria. Gesú . . . Maria. "


HIS last word - THE last word - is still

MARY!